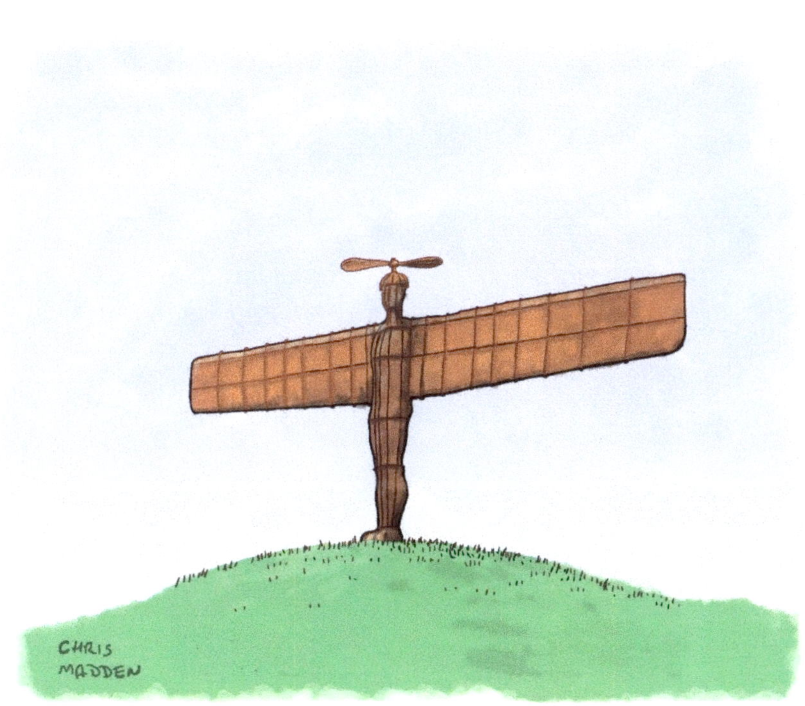
CHRIS
MADDEN

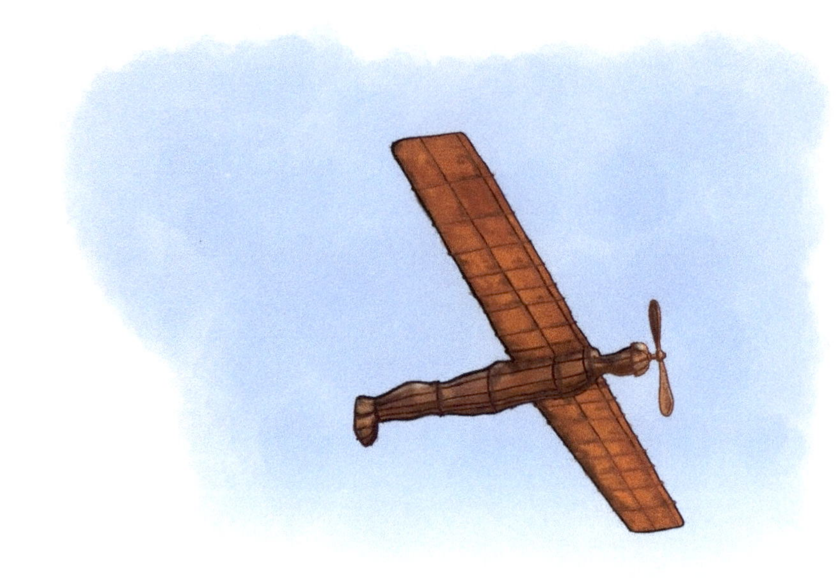

Never Judge an Artwork

Till You Know What it's Worth

and other cartoons about art

Chris Madden

Inkline Press

Published by Inkline Press.
www.inklinepress.com

Copyright © Chris Madden 2019

All rights reserved. No part of this book may be reproduced in any form, stored in any retrieval system, or transmitted in any form by any means, electronic, mechanical, photocopy, recording, or otherwise, without prior written permission of the publisher.

For permission to use any of the cartoons please go to
www.inklinepress.com/permission
To obtain prints of cartoons please go to
www.chrismadden.co.uk/prints
Author's websites:
Cartoons: www.chrismadden.co.uk
Art: www.christophermadden.art

Versions of the cartoons on the following pages
have been published in the following magazines
Oldie: frontispiece
Private Eye: 13, 32, 44
Spectator: 3, 89
Philosophy Now: 25, 92

ISBN 978-0-9548551-7-8

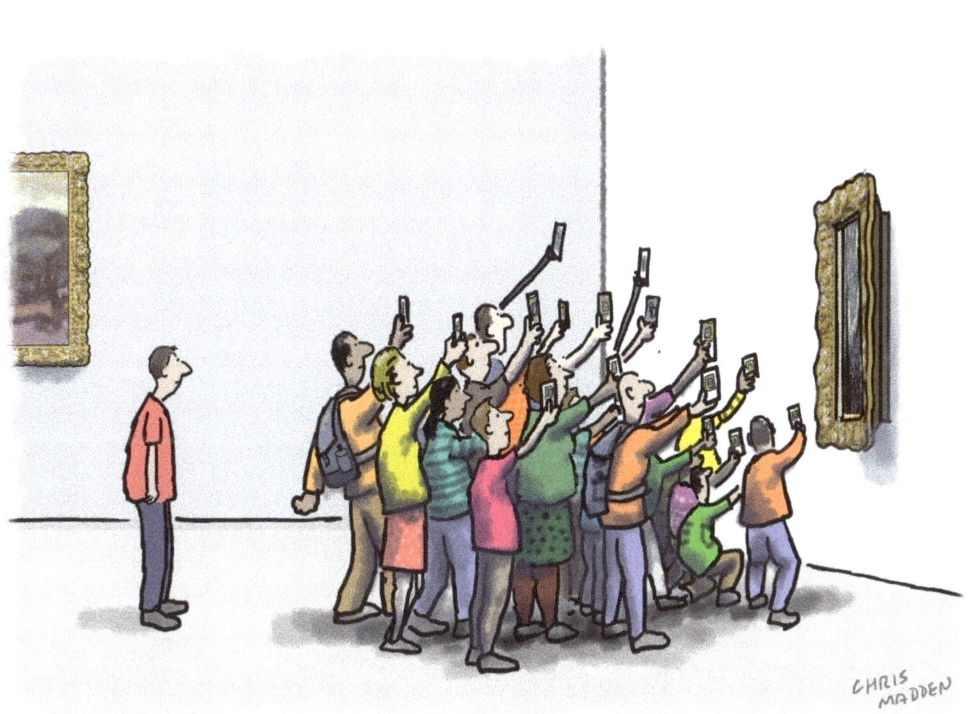
CHRIS MADDEN

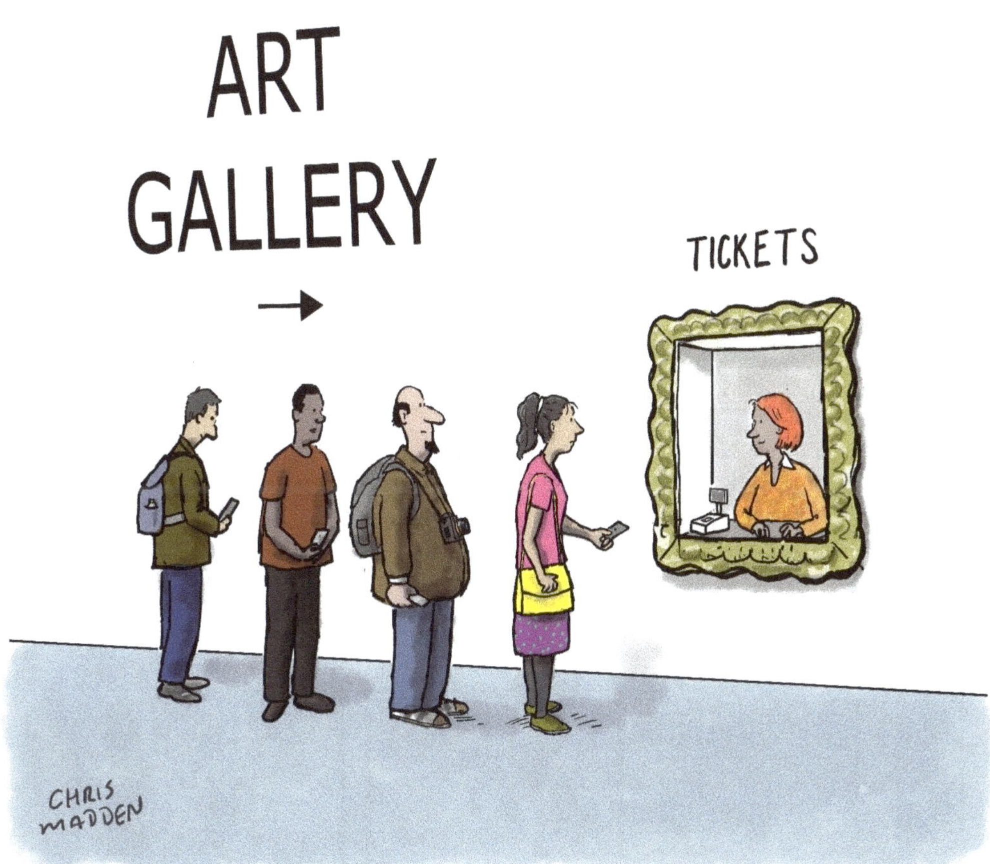
ART
GALLERY
TICKETS
CHRIS
MADDEN

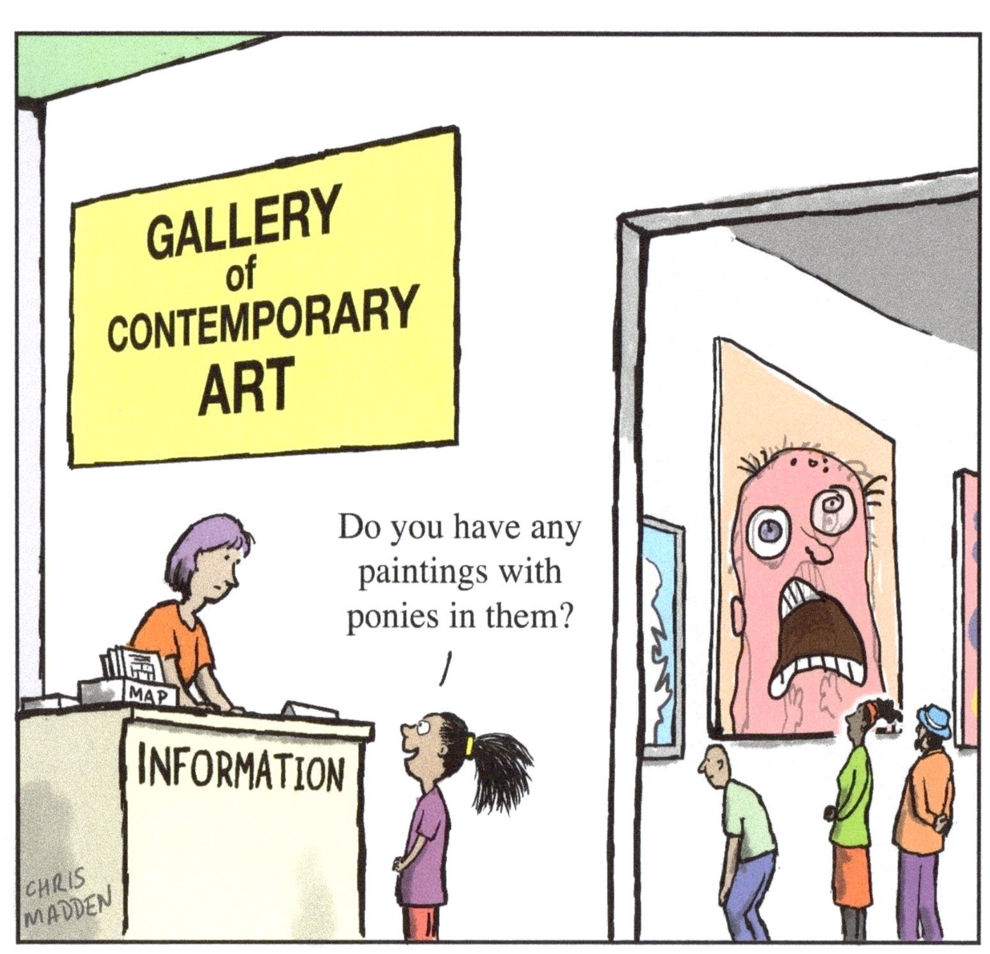
GALLERY
of
CONTEMPORARY
ART
Do you have any paintings with ponies in them?
MAP
INFORMATION
CHRIS MADDEN

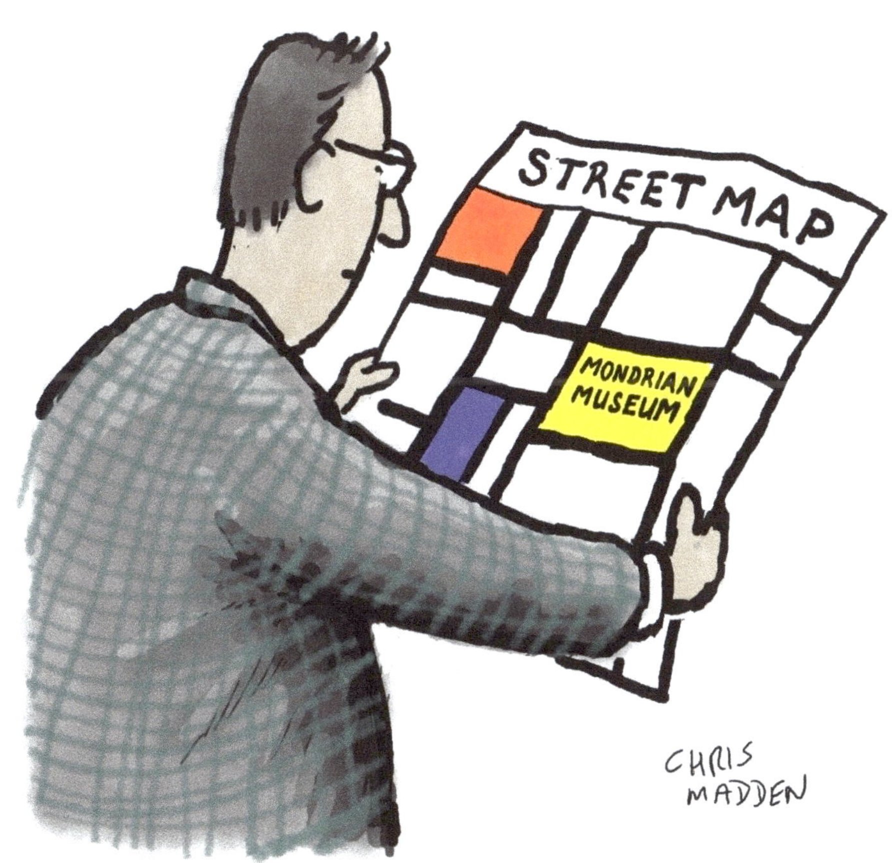
STREET MAP
MONDRIAN MUSEUM
CHRIS MADDEN

I'M TRYING TO EXPLORE MY DARK SIDE,
BUT I'M BEGINNING TO WORRY THAT
I MAY NOT HAVE ONE.

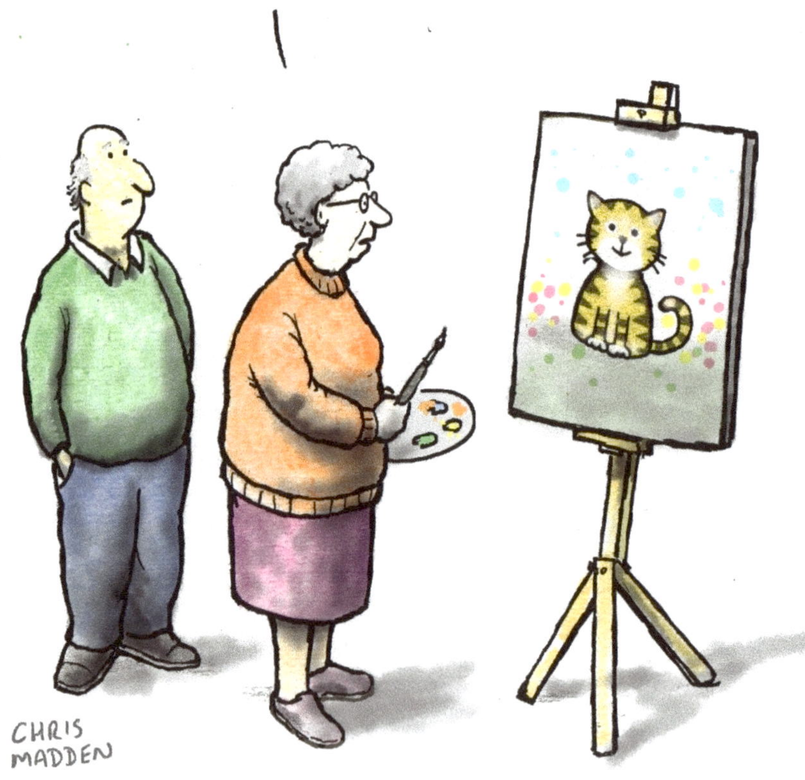

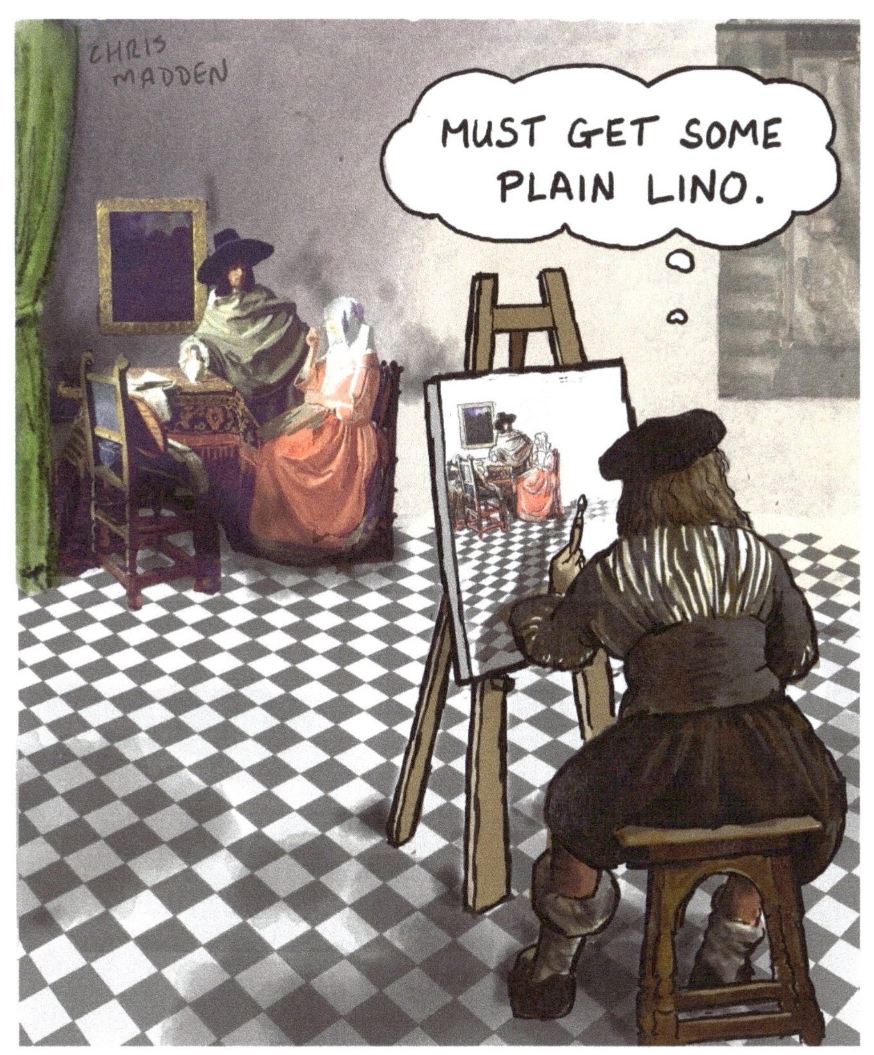
CHRIS MADDEN
MUST GET SOME PLAIN LINO.

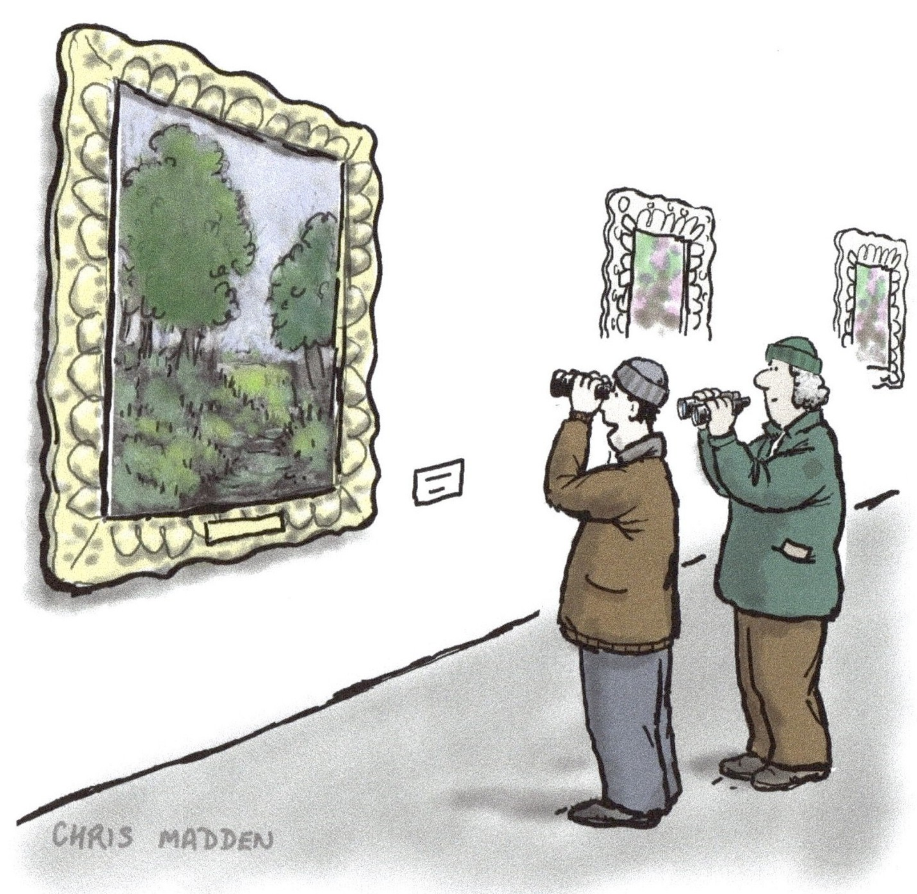

“In the tree on the left –
a greater spotted woodpecker!”

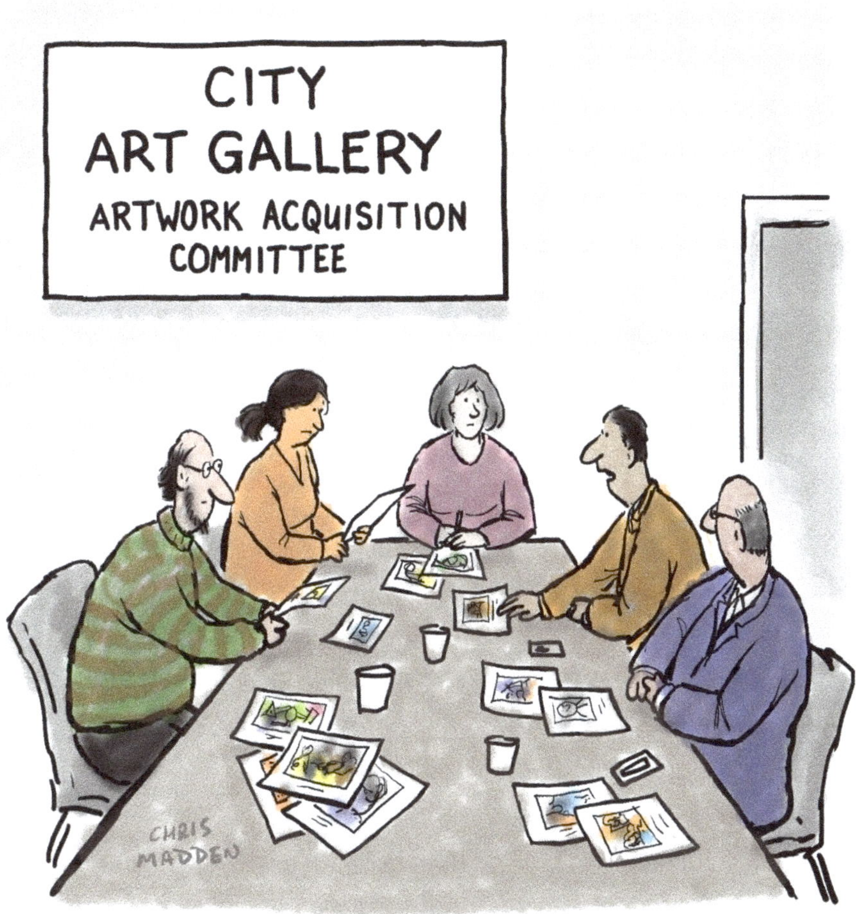

"It may indeed be a hugely significant example of early 18th century Flemish art that would enhance the gallery's collection immeasurably, but as head of merchandising I have to ask 'What would it look like on a fridge magnet?'."

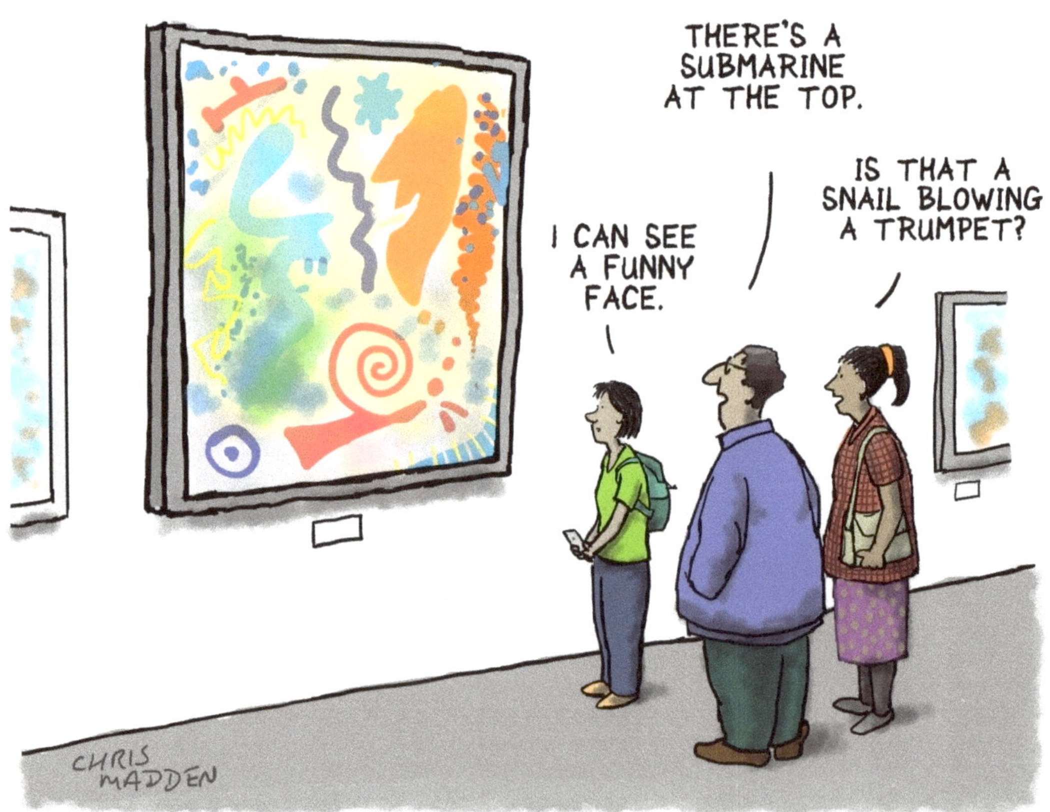

The curse that afflicts abstract art.

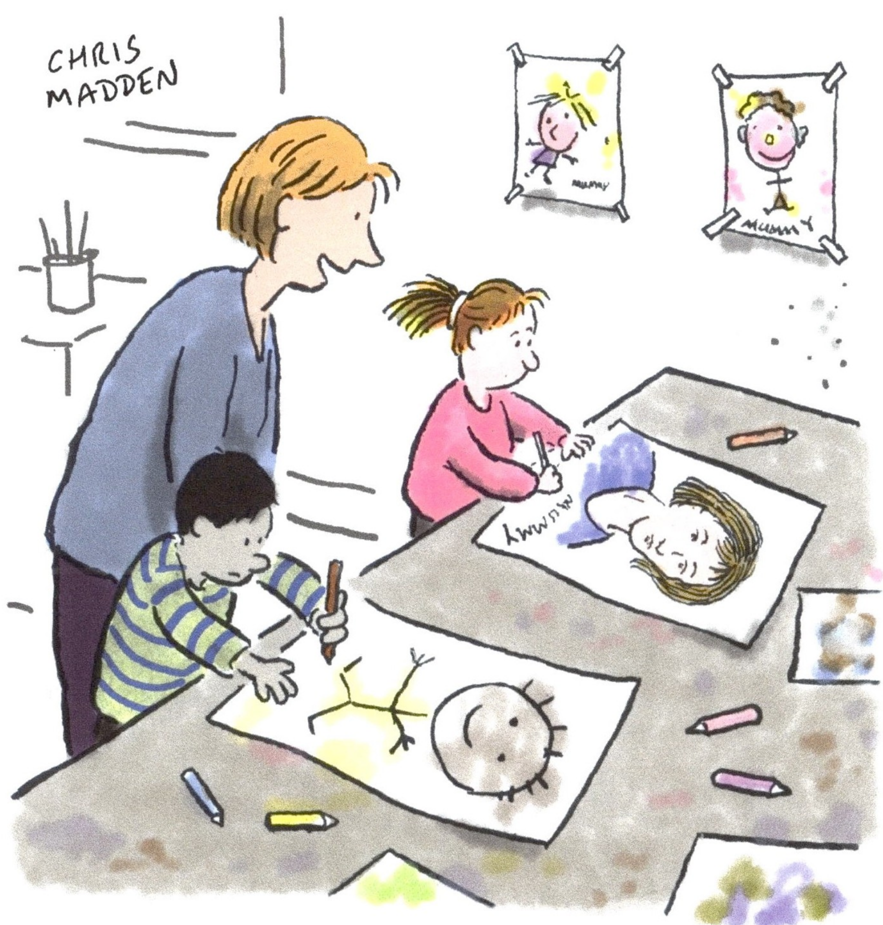

"That's a *lovely* drawing, Sophie! Now let's draw one with Mummy's head like a big round balloon."

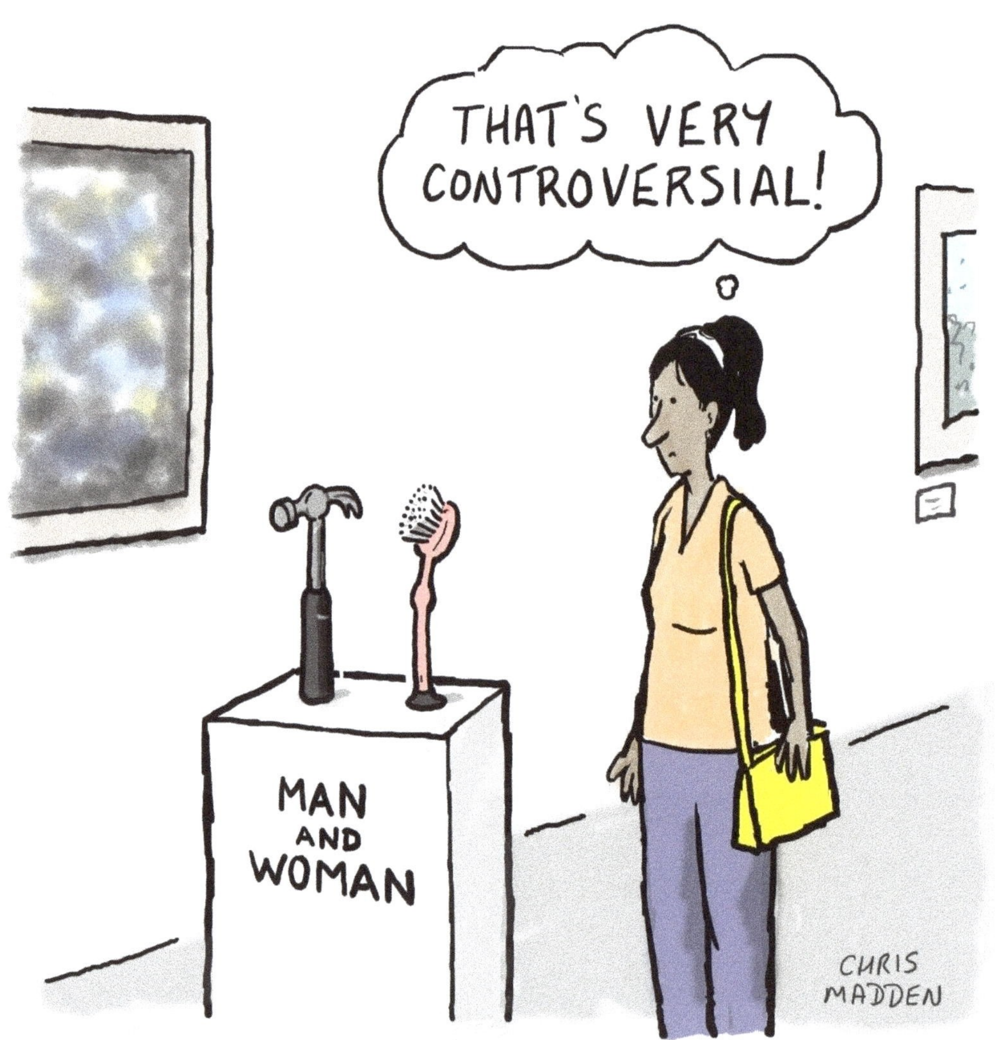
THAT'S VERY CONTROVERSIAL!
MAN AND WOMAN
CHRIS MADDEN

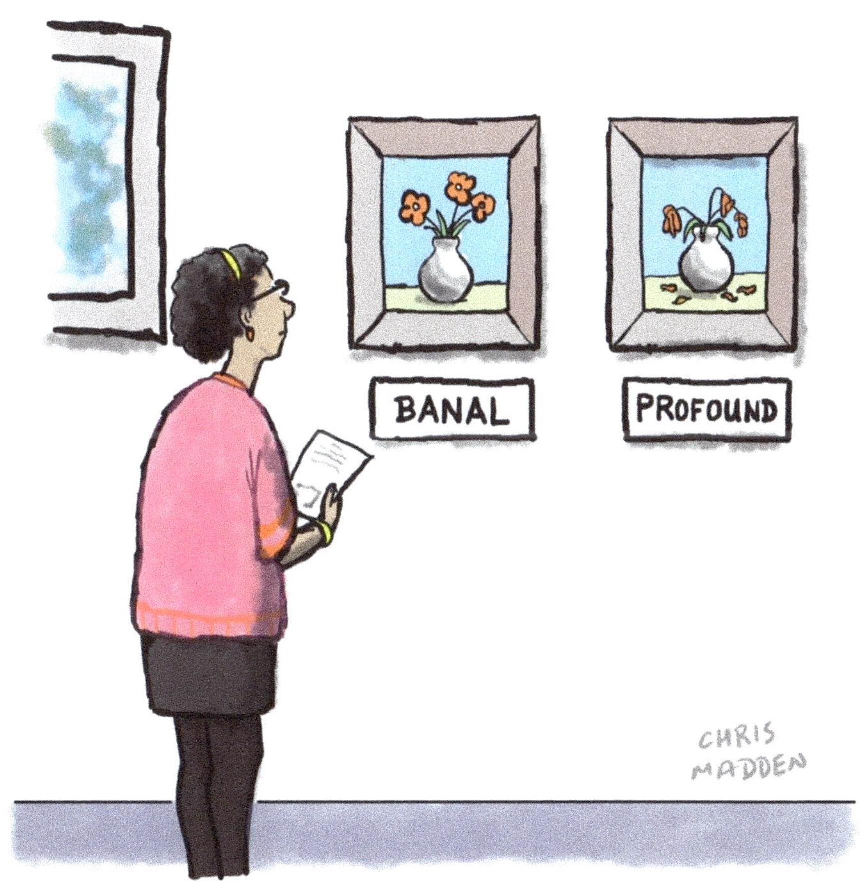
BANAL
PROFOUND
CHRIS MADDEN

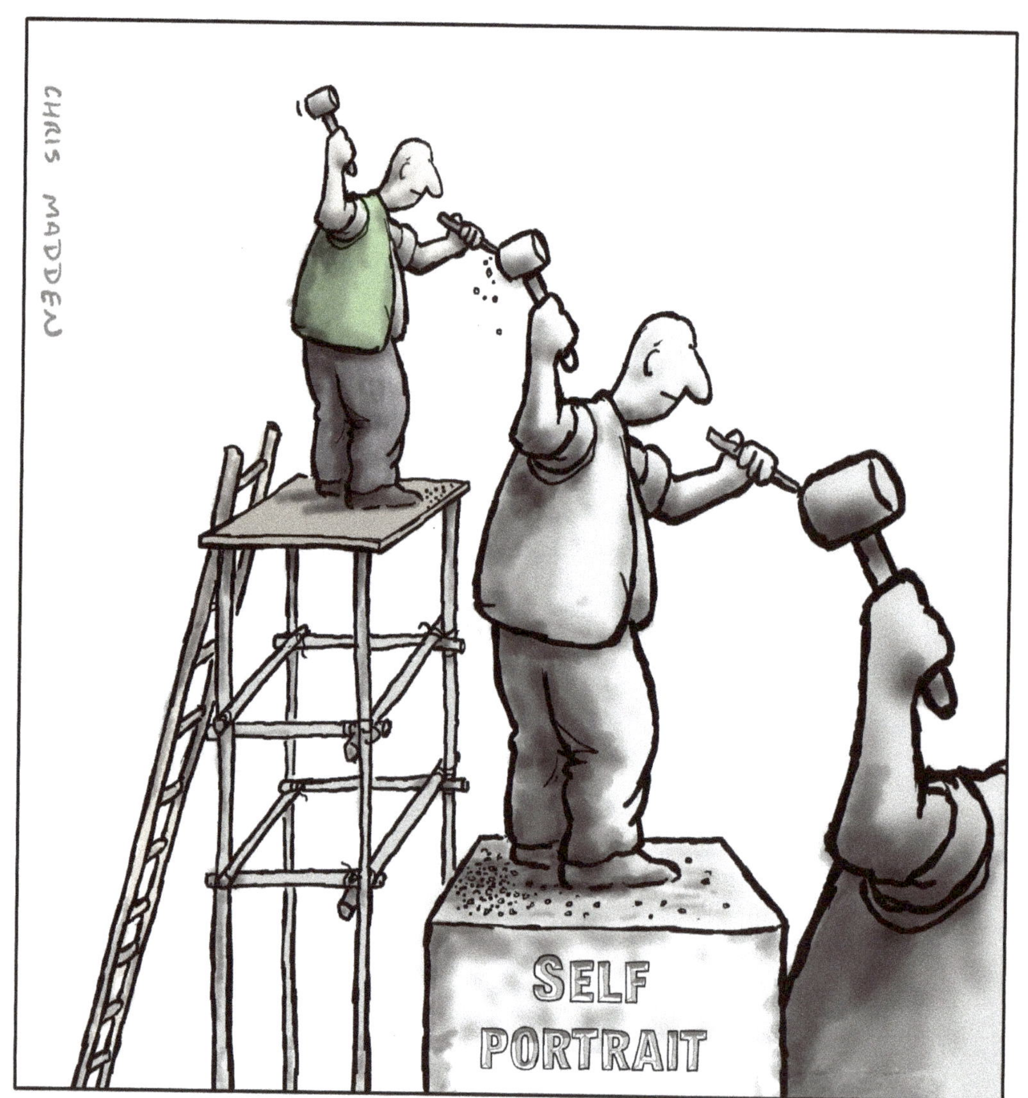
CHRIS MADDEN
SELF
PORTRAIT

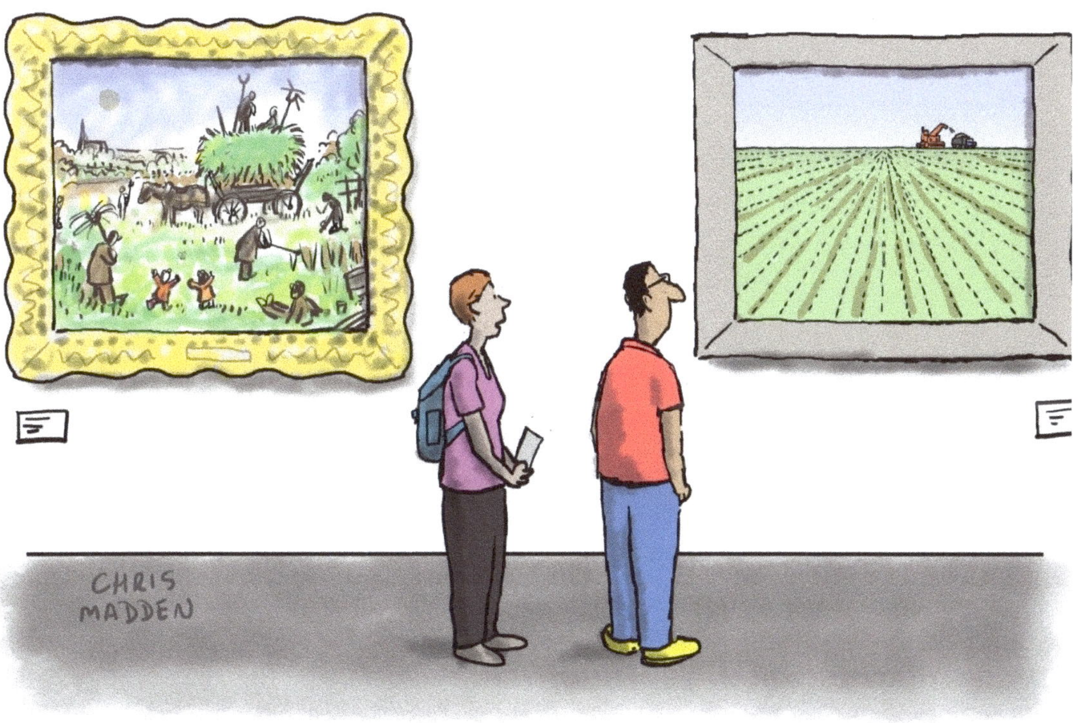

"The pastoral painting genre has definitely lost something over the years."

LOBSTER TELEPHONE

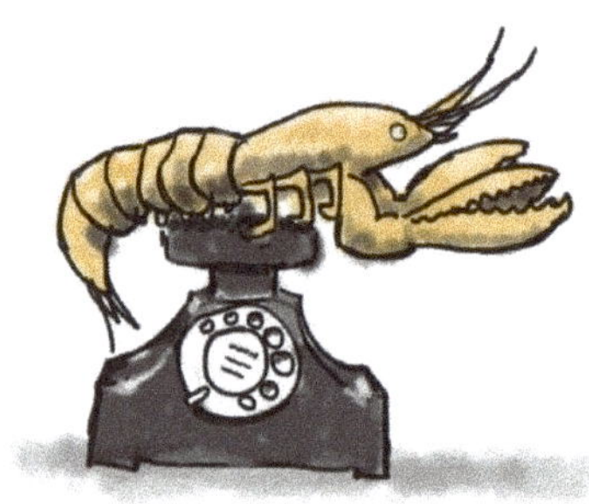

SHRIMP MOBILE PHONE

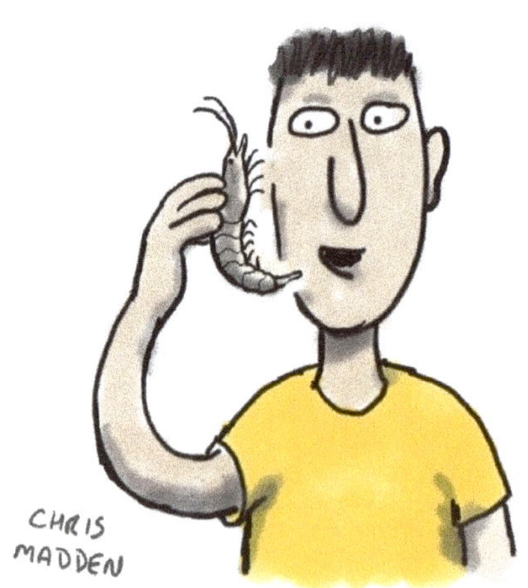

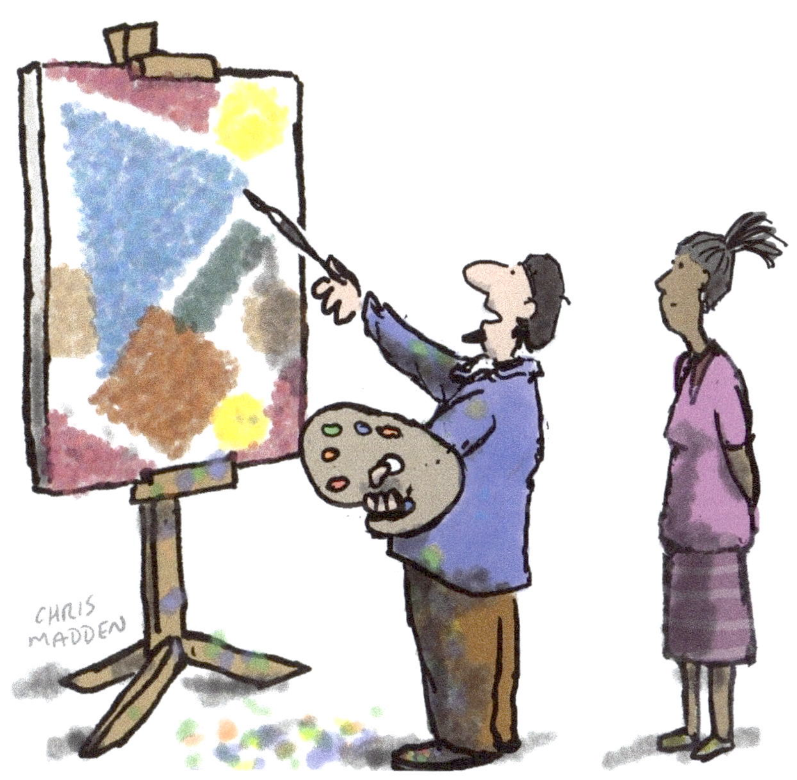

"While I'm alive I like the idea of my work living on when I'm dead – but when I'm dead I probably won't care one way or the other."

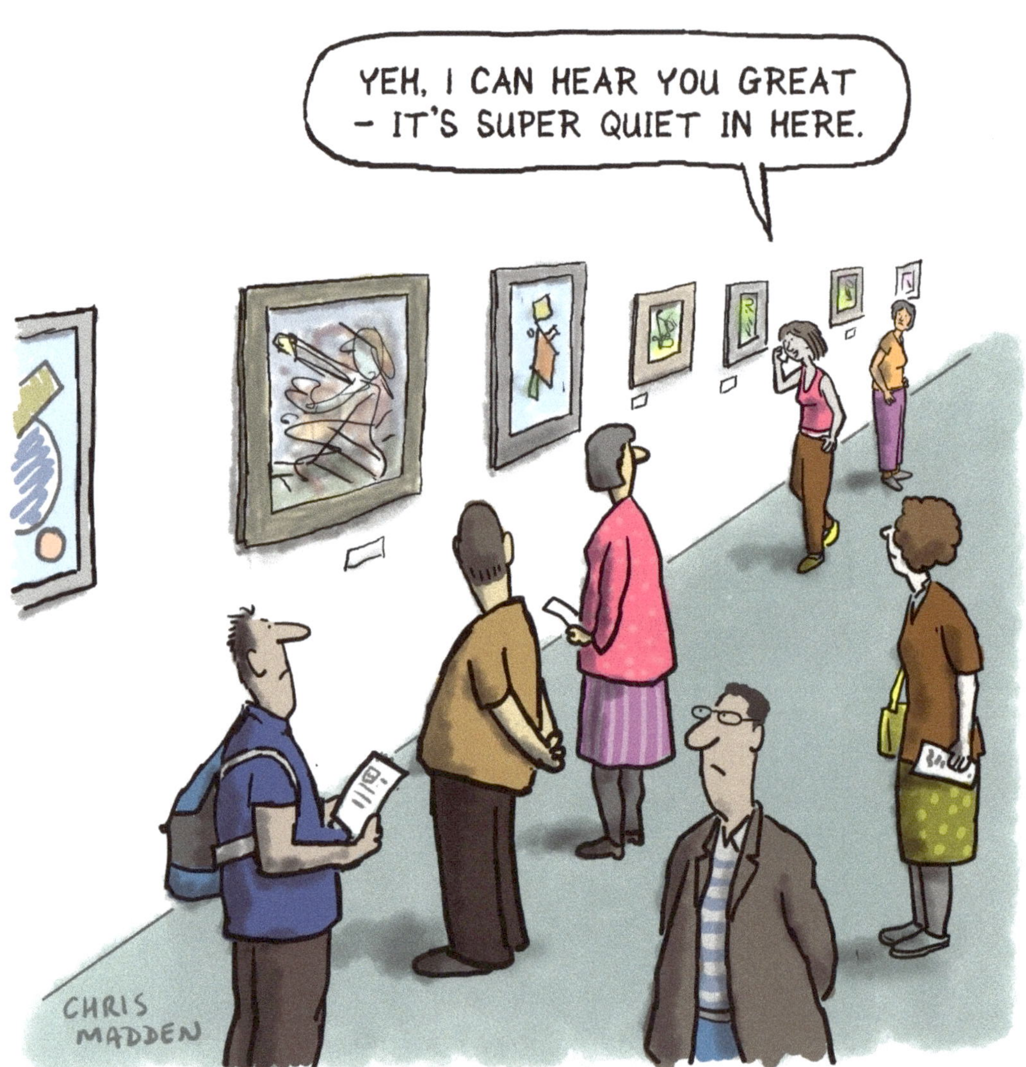
YEH, I CAN HEAR YOU GREAT - IT'S SUPER QUIET IN HERE.
CHRIS MADDEN

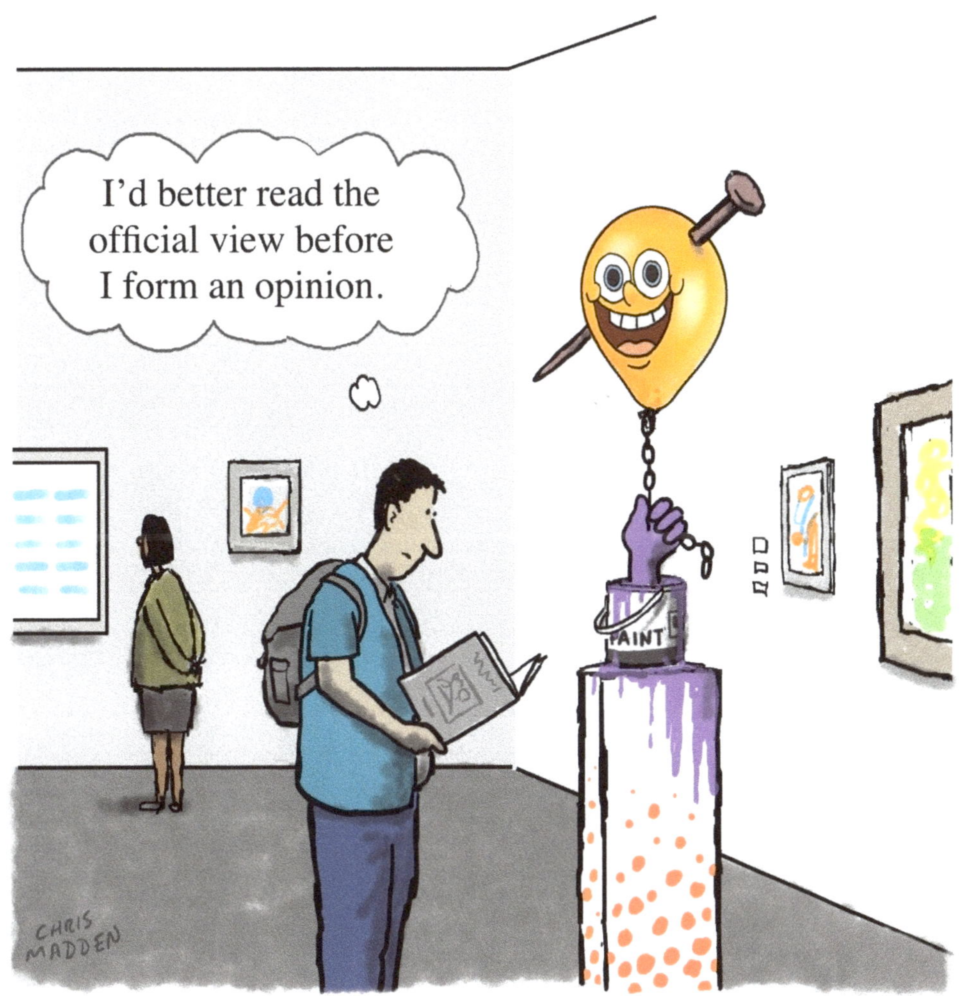
I'd better read the official view before I form an opinion.
PAINT
CHRIS MADDEN

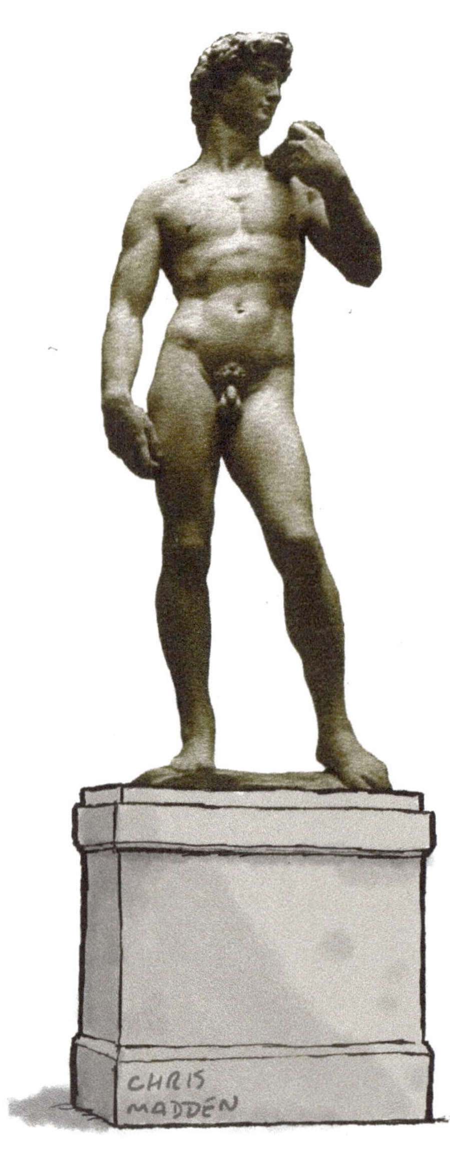

“If this is his David,
I’d love to see his
Goliath!”

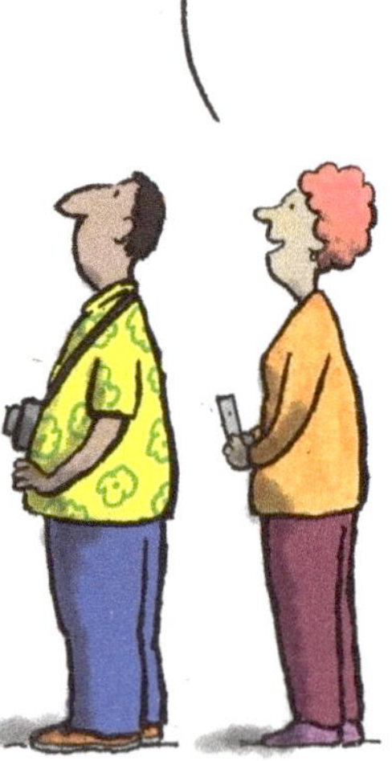

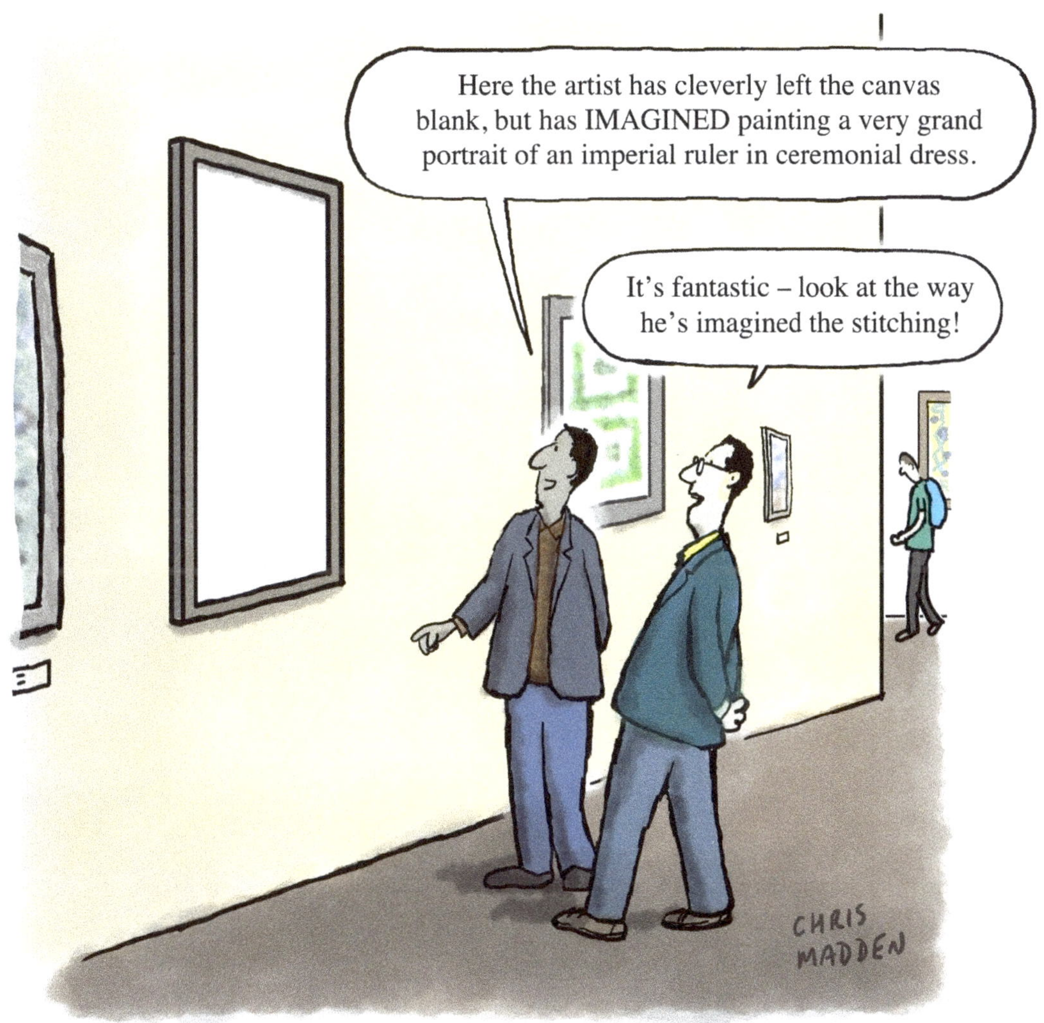

The Emperor's New Clothes

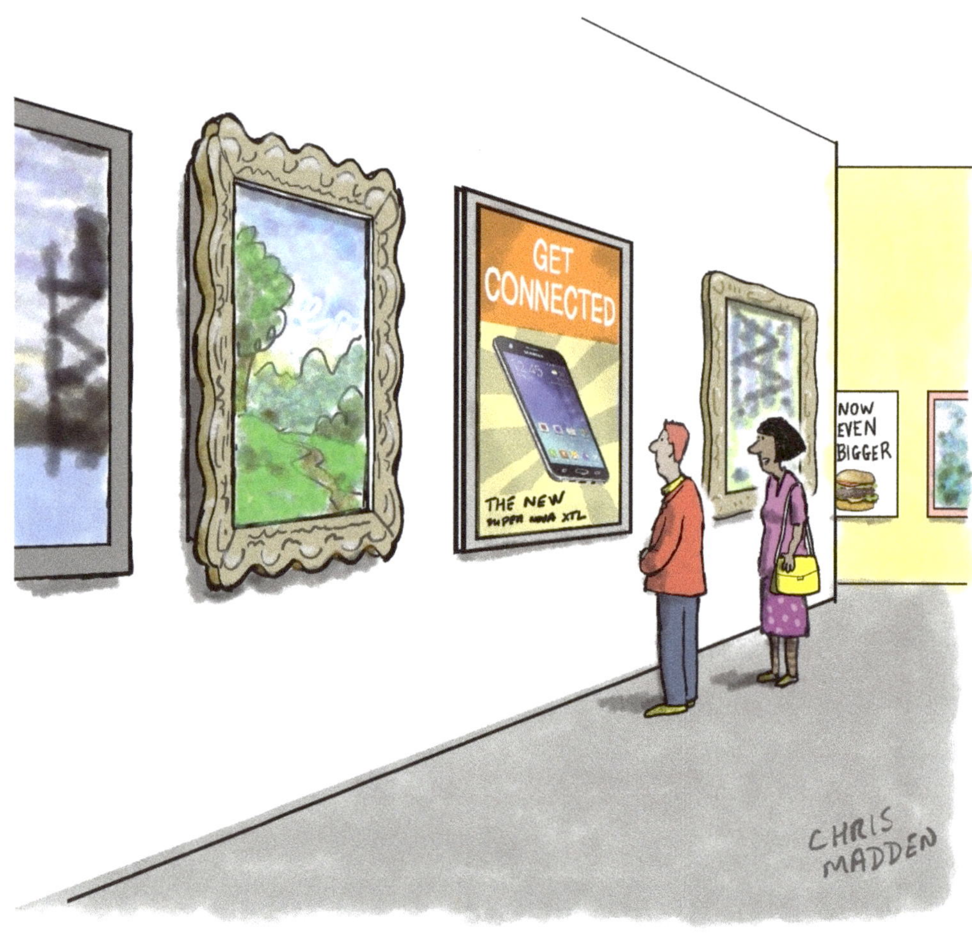

"It's the new financial model for the gallery – every fourth image is an advert."

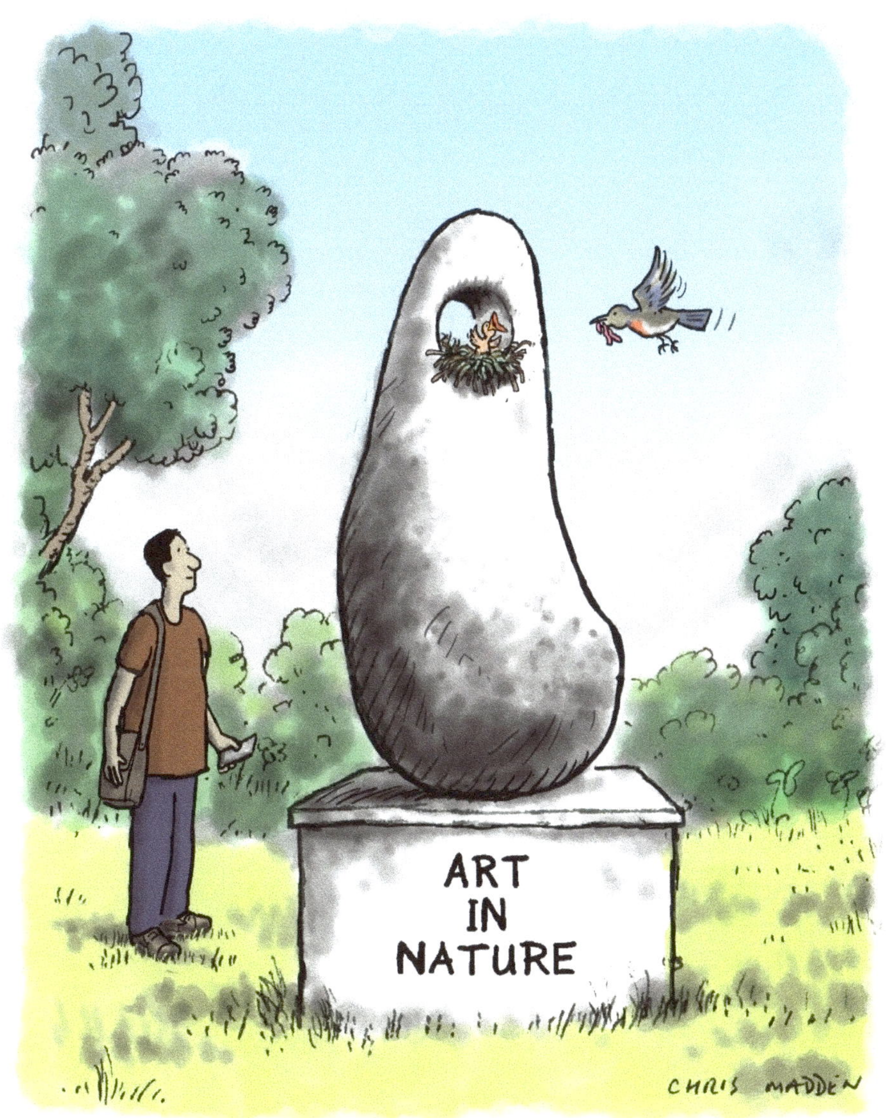
ART
IN
NATURE
CHRIS MADDEN

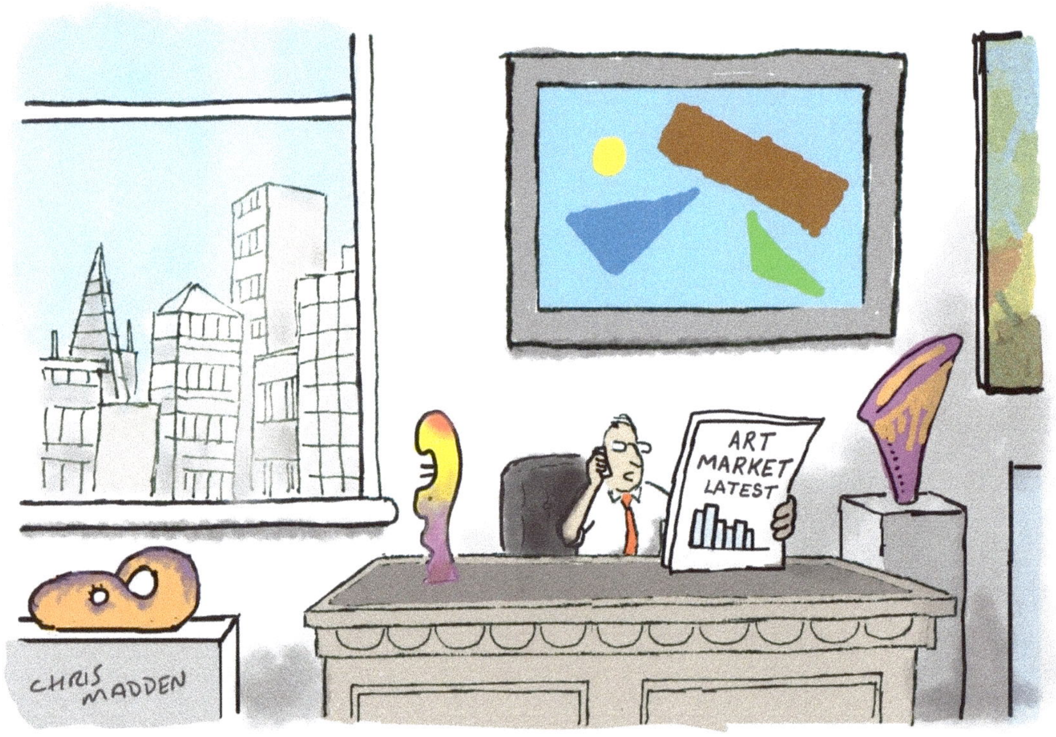

"Sell abstract expressionism. Buy concrete conceptualism."

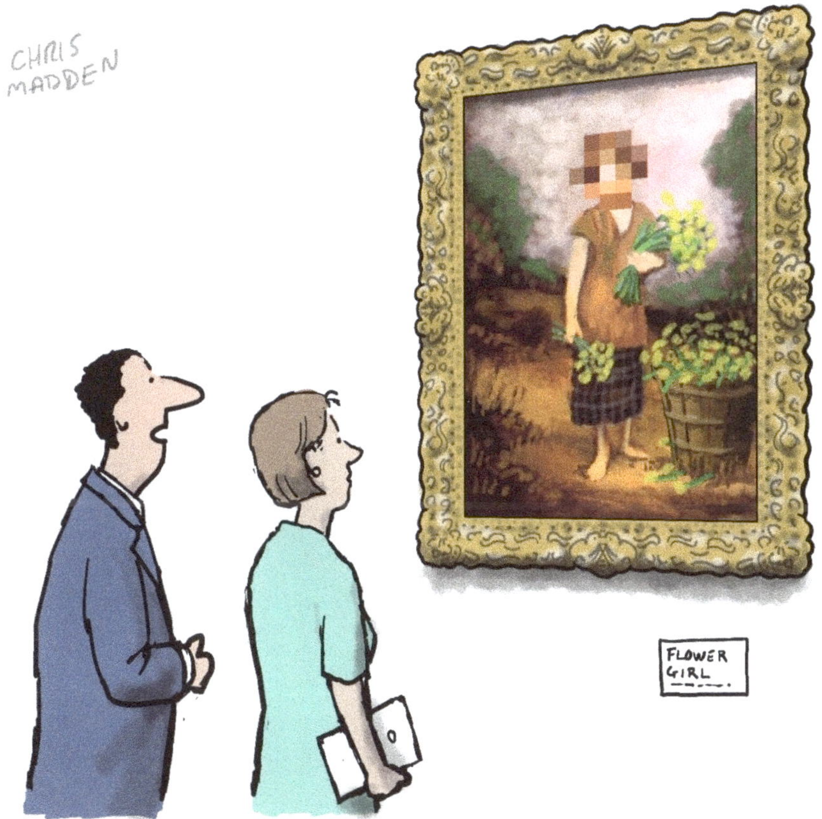

“When we had this one restored we took the opportunity to make it comply with the new regulations on the depiction of children.”

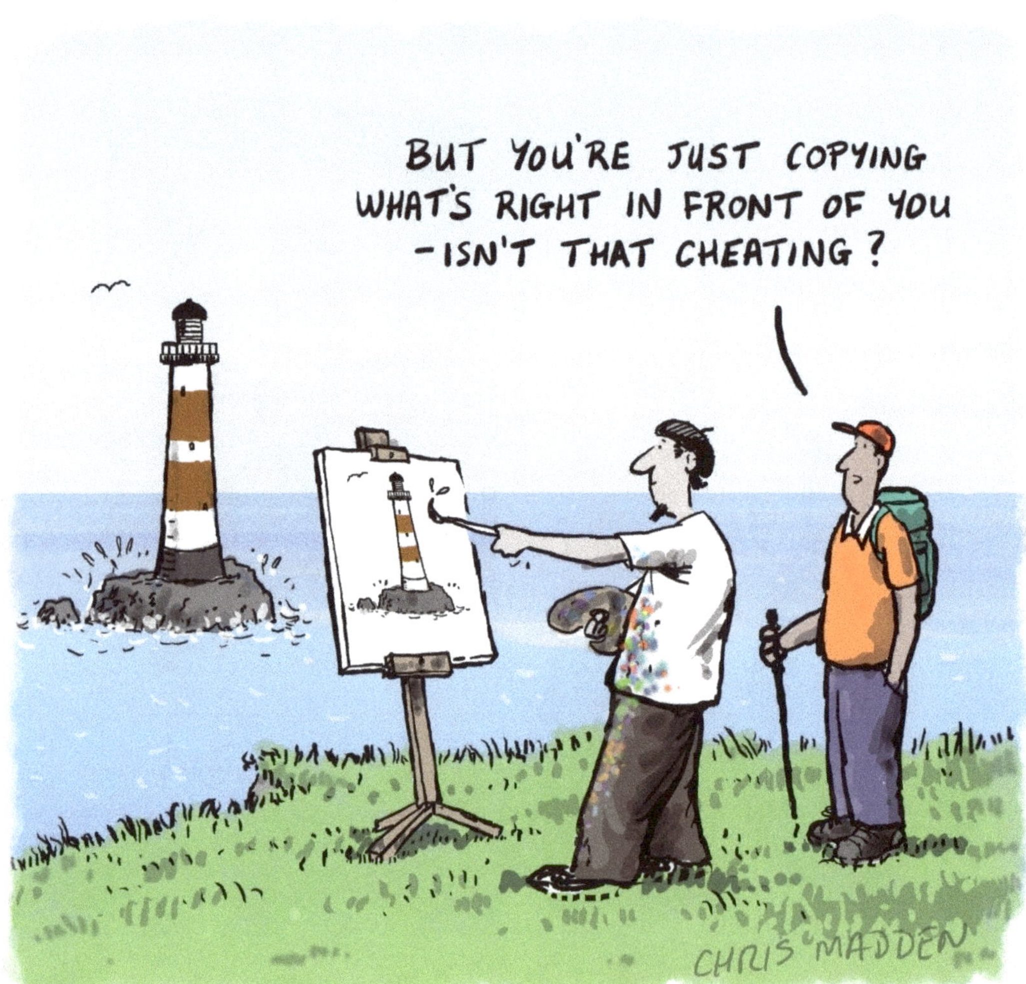
BUT YOU'RE JUST COPYING WHAT'S RIGHT IN FRONT OF YOU - ISN'T THAT CHEATING?
CHRIS MADDEN

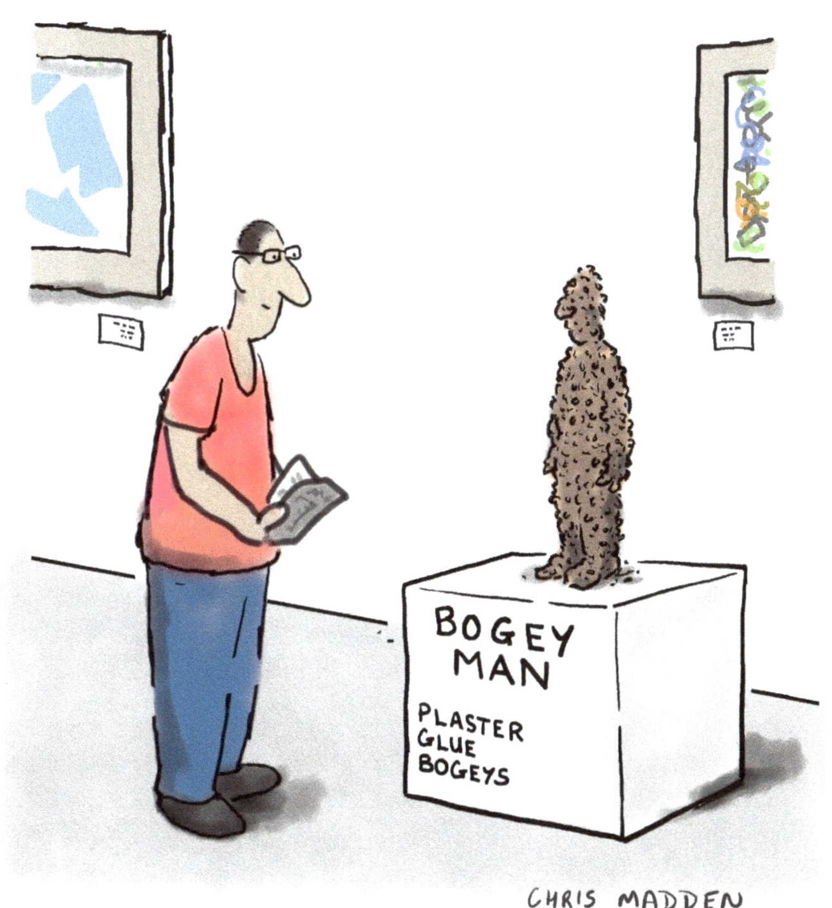
BOGEY
MAN
PLASTER
GLUE
BOGEYS
CHRIS MADDEN

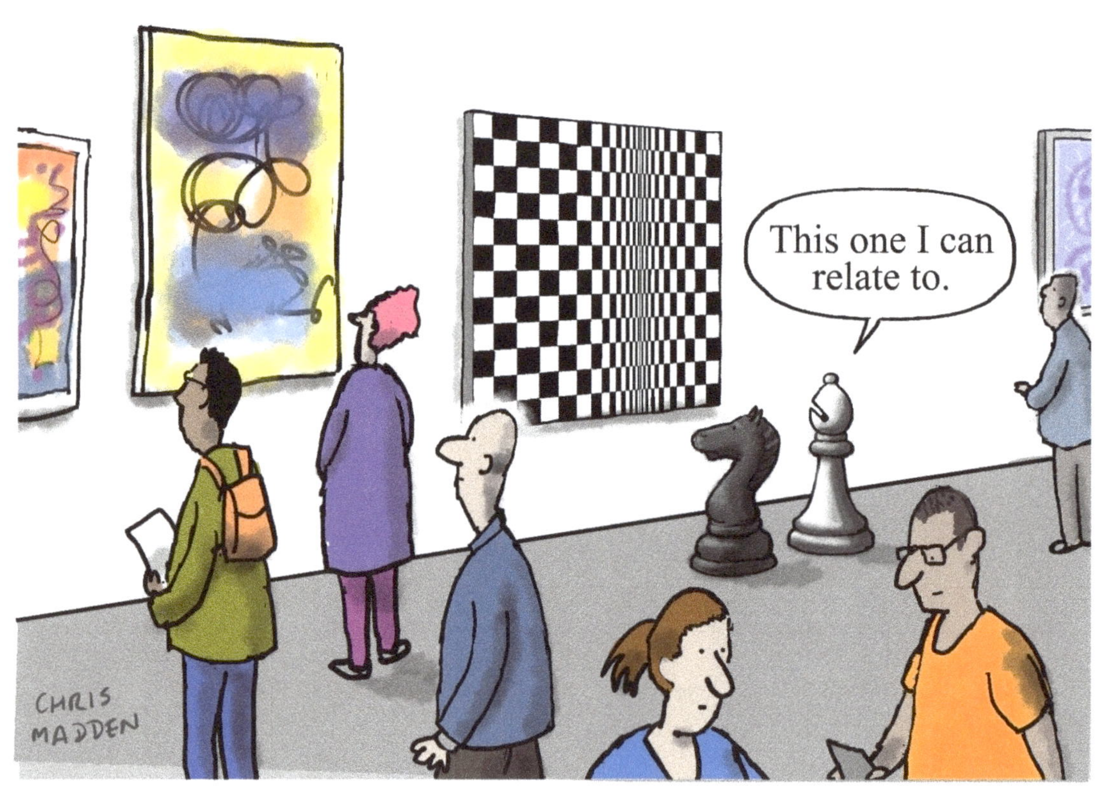
This one I can relate to.
CHRIS MADDEN

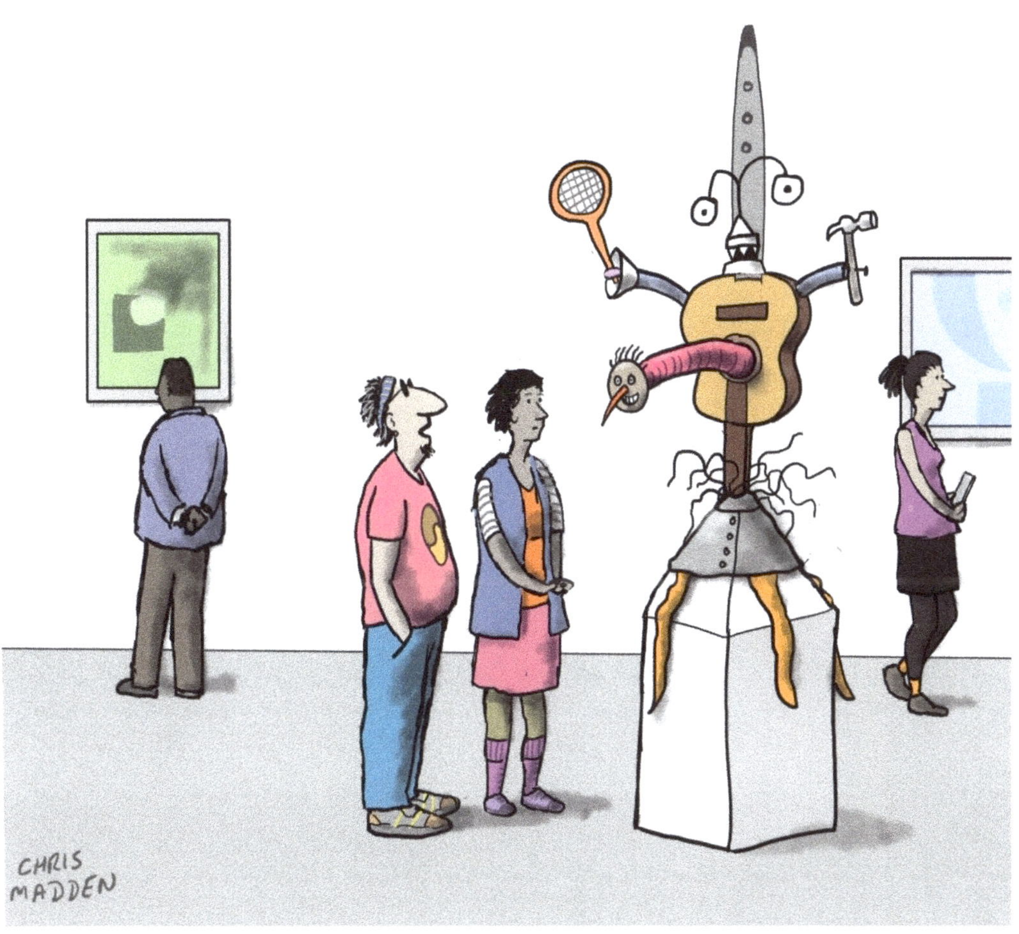

“I like the sort of art that no-one understands – mainly because as a result nobody realises that I don’t understand it either.”

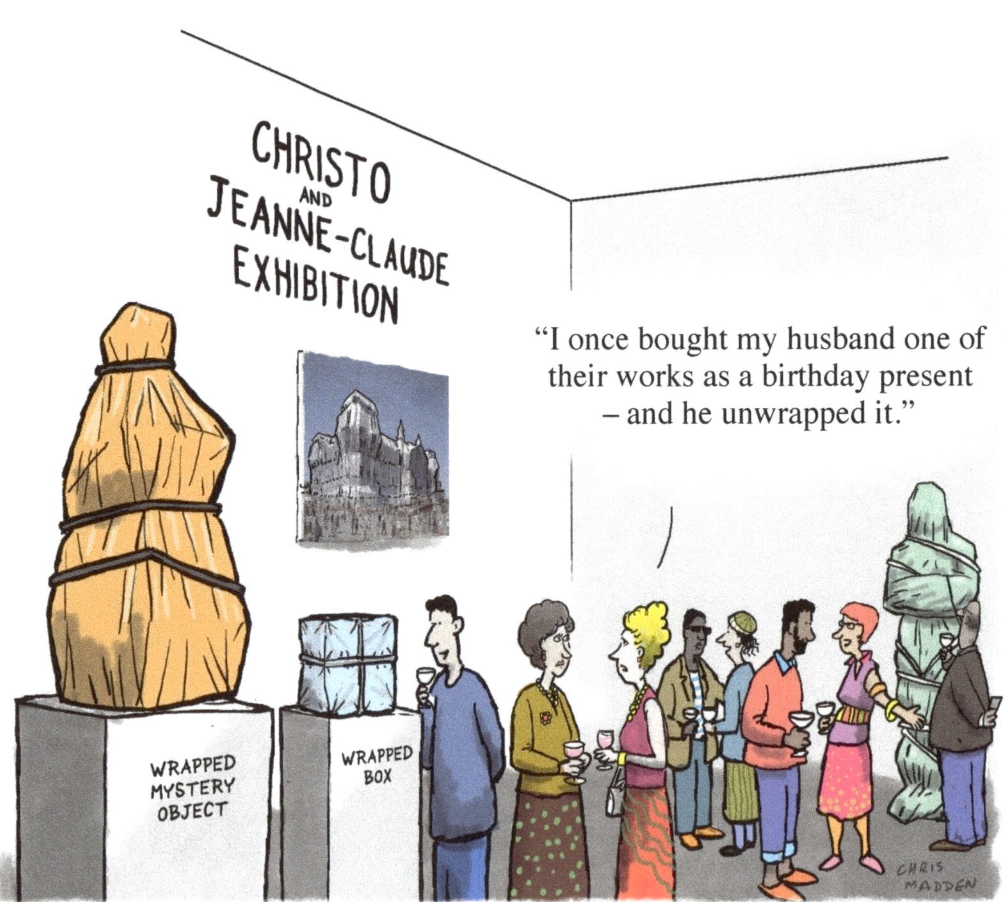
CHRISTO
AND
JEANNE-CLAUDE
EXHIBITION
"I once bought my husband one of
their works as a birthday present
– and he unwrapped it."
WRAPPED
MYSTERY
OBJECT
WRAPPED
BOX
CHRIS
MADDEN

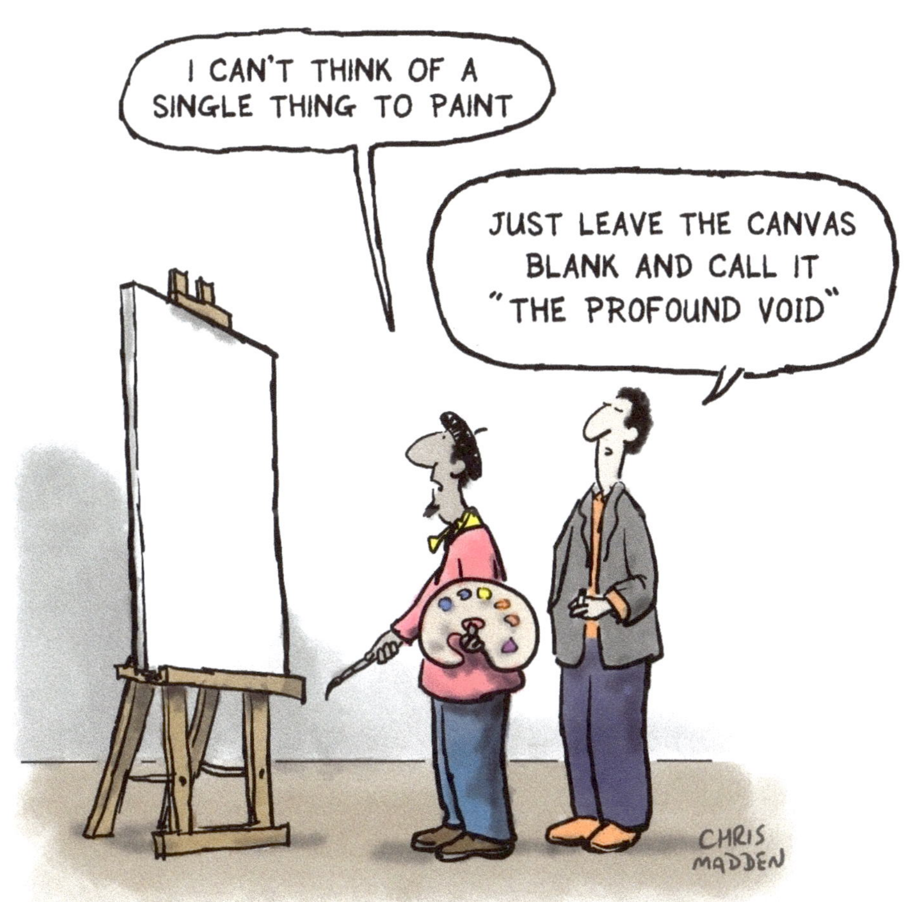
I CAN'T THINK OF A SINGLE THING TO PAINT
JUST LEAVE THE CANVAS BLANK AND CALL IT "THE PROFOUND VOID"
CHRIS MADDEN

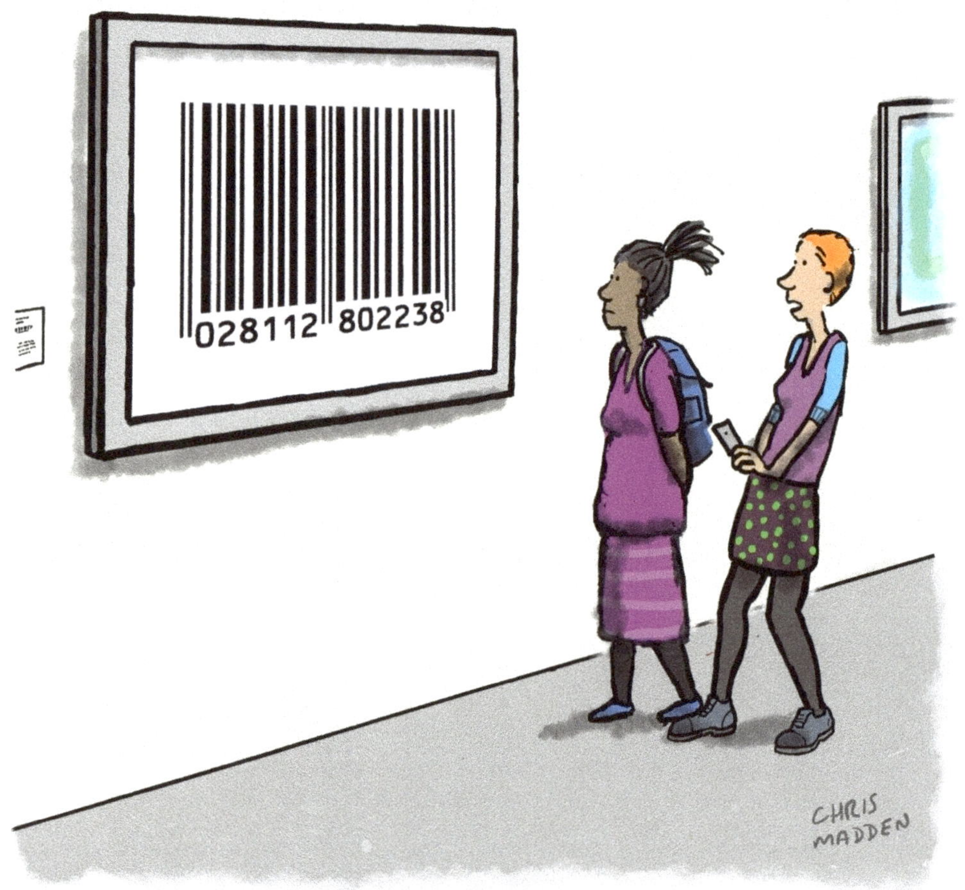

"I'm not sure whether this is her *Tetley Teabags* piece or her *Waitrose Colombian Coffee Beans*."

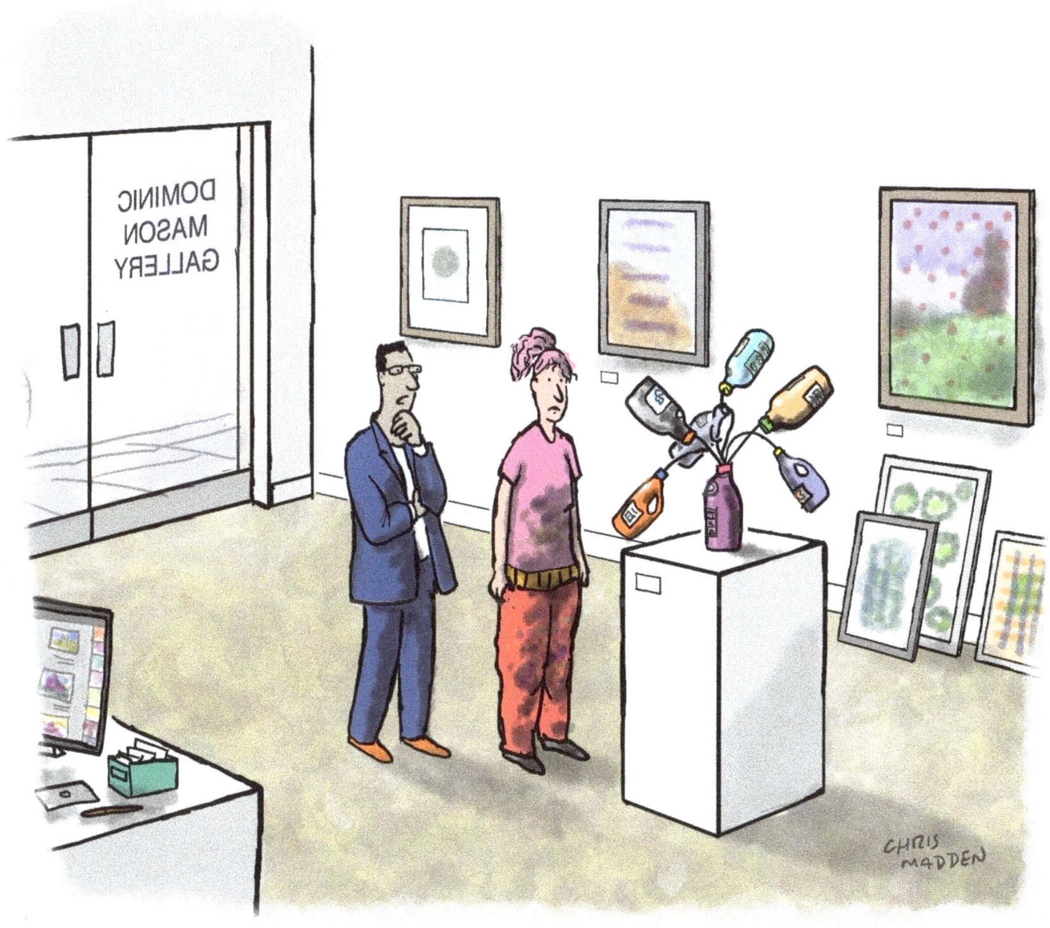

"You've certainly created a wonderful statement about the environment crisis, Olivia, but collectors may have issues about the fact that it's a hundred percent biodegradable."

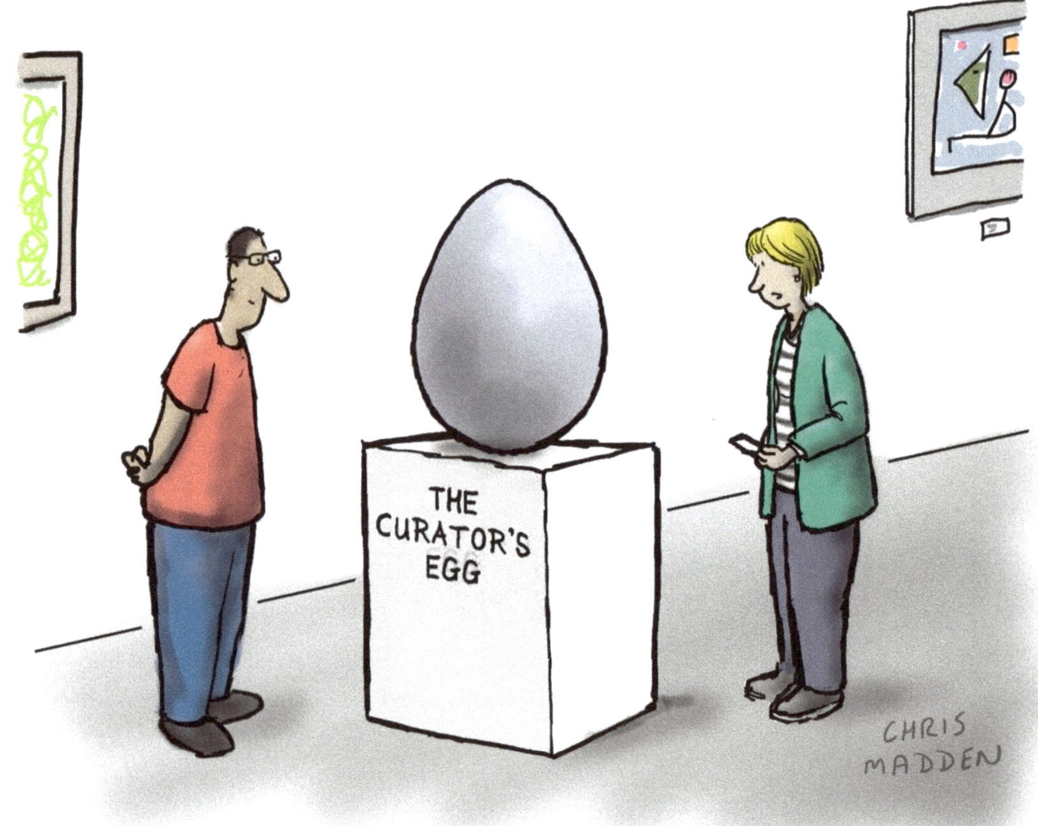

"Parts of it are excellent."

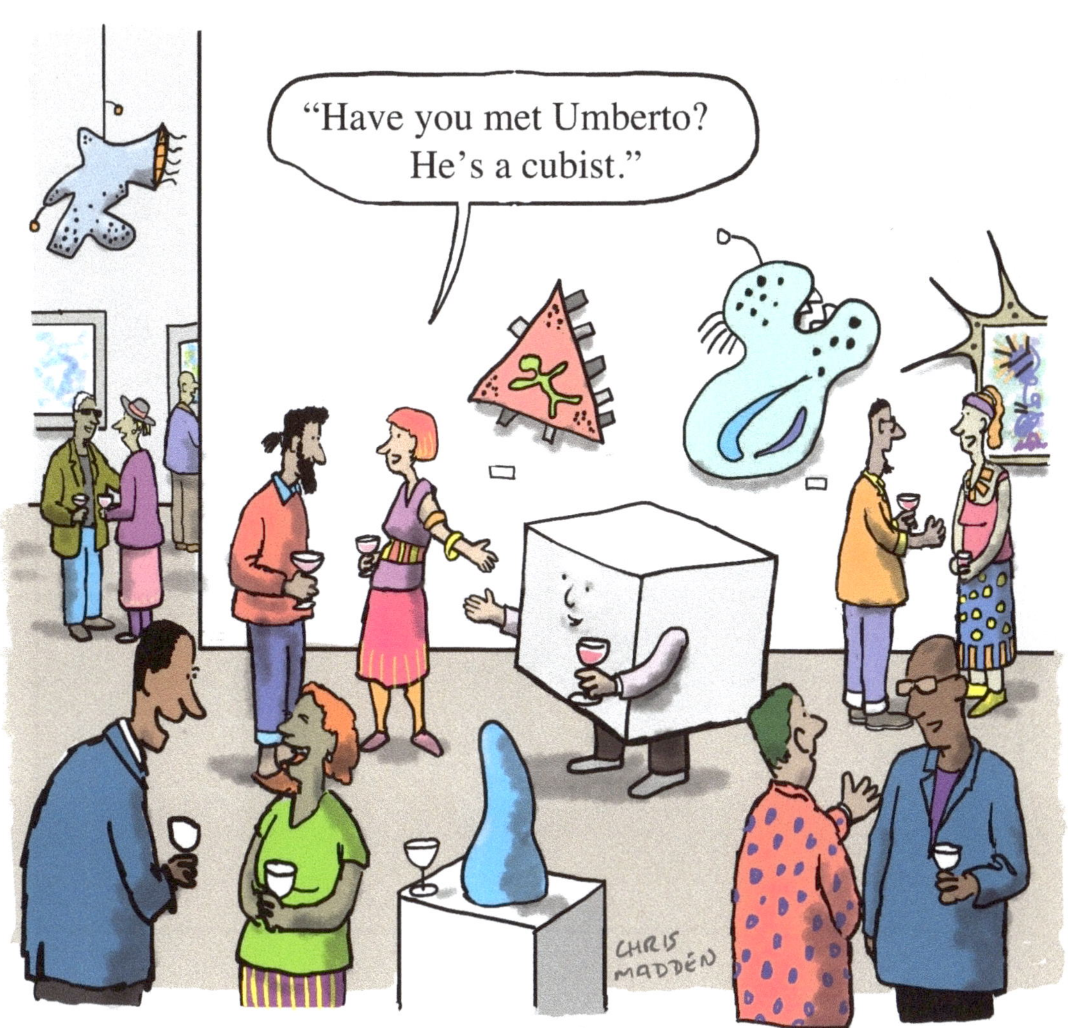
"Have you met Umberto? He's a cubist."
CHRIS MADDEN

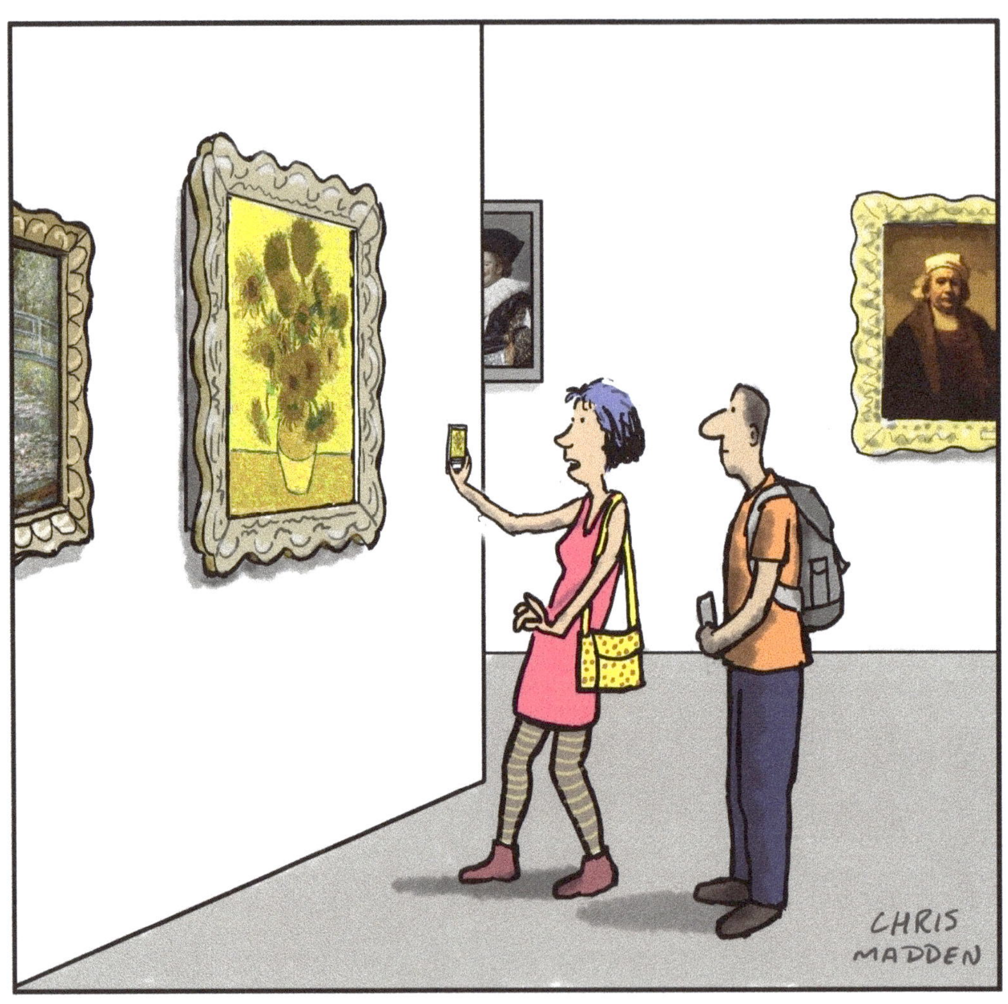

"I've got this great new app – I point my phone at a painting and it tells me its current market value."

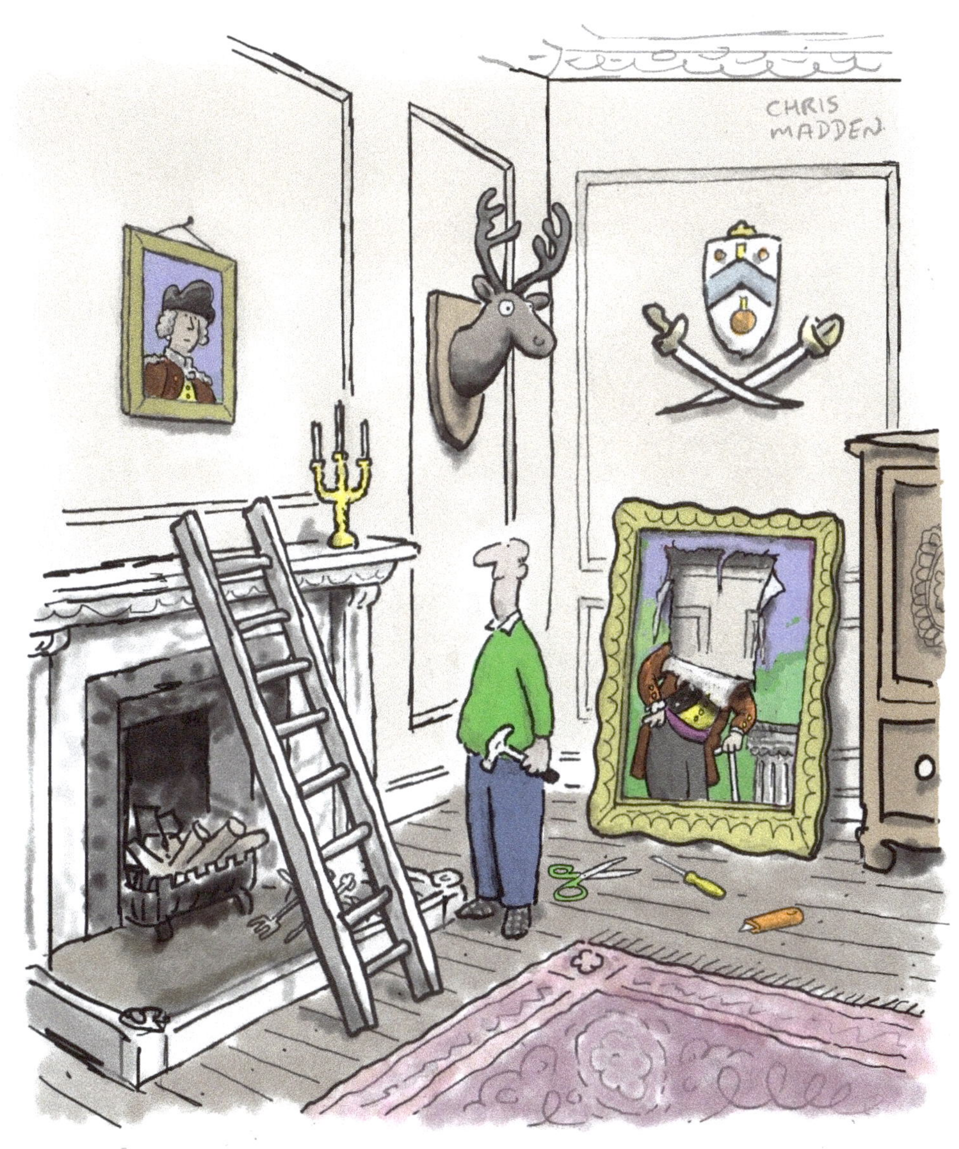
CHRIS MADDEN

"I sometimes think that art galleries are becoming too entertainment orientated."

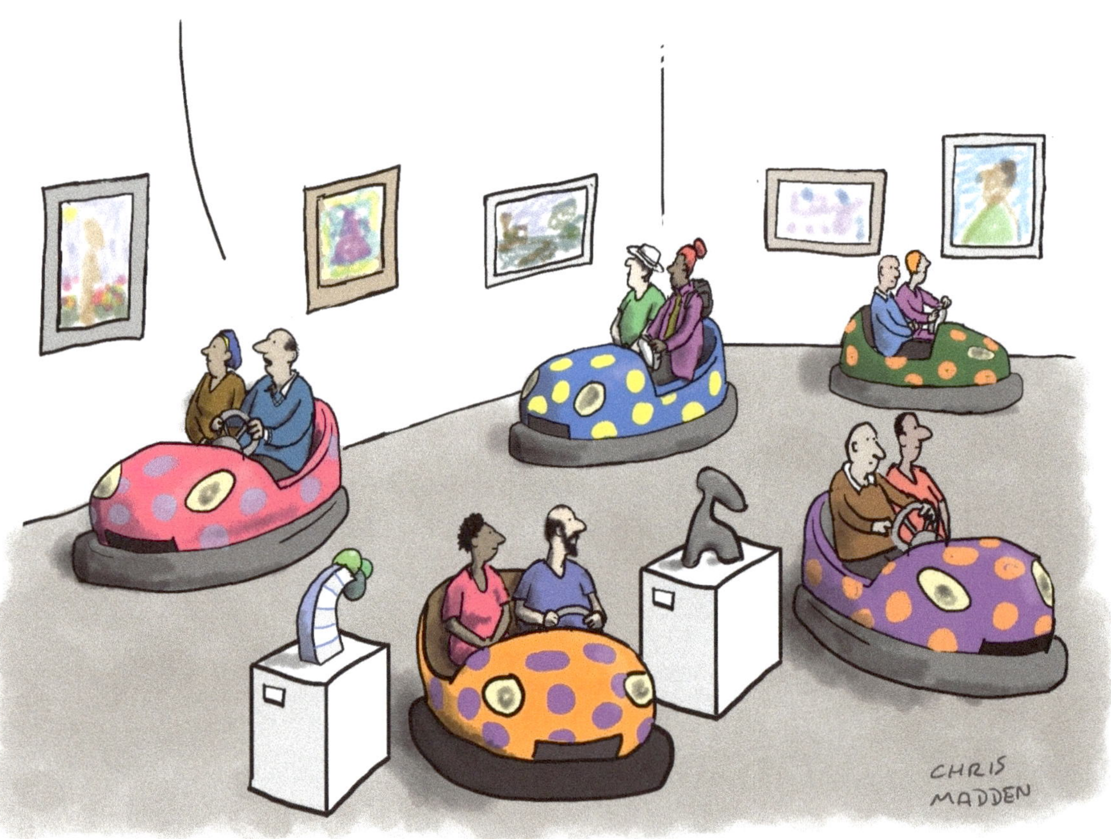

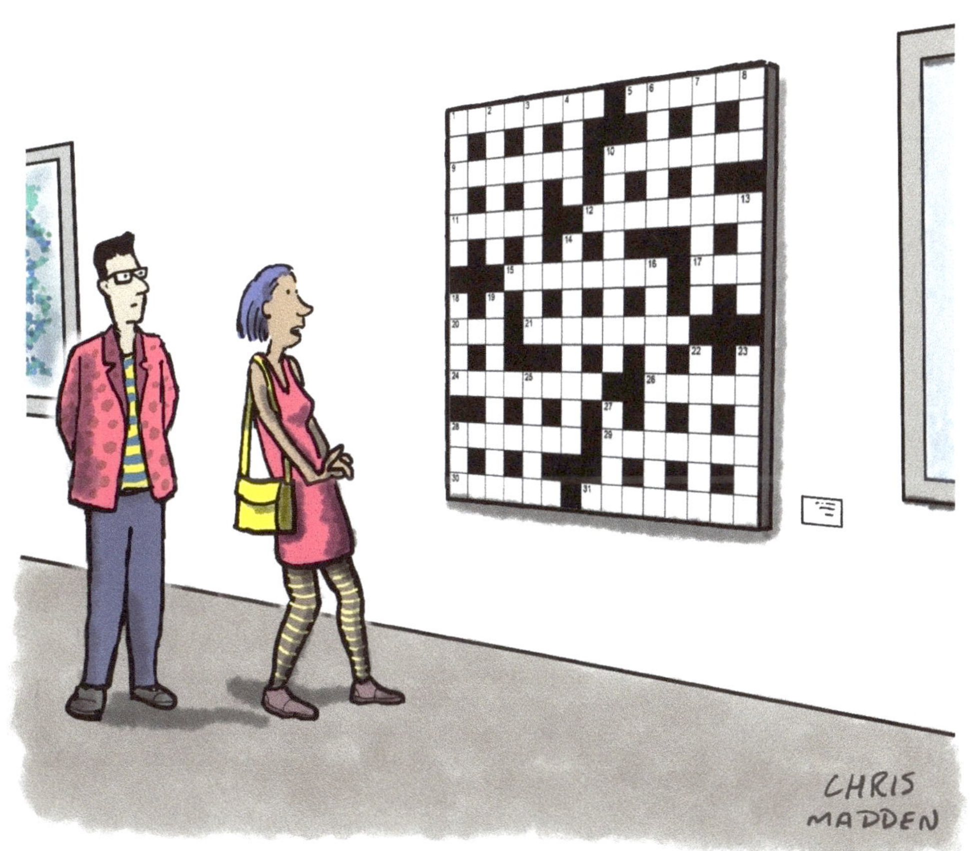

"It's very cryptic."

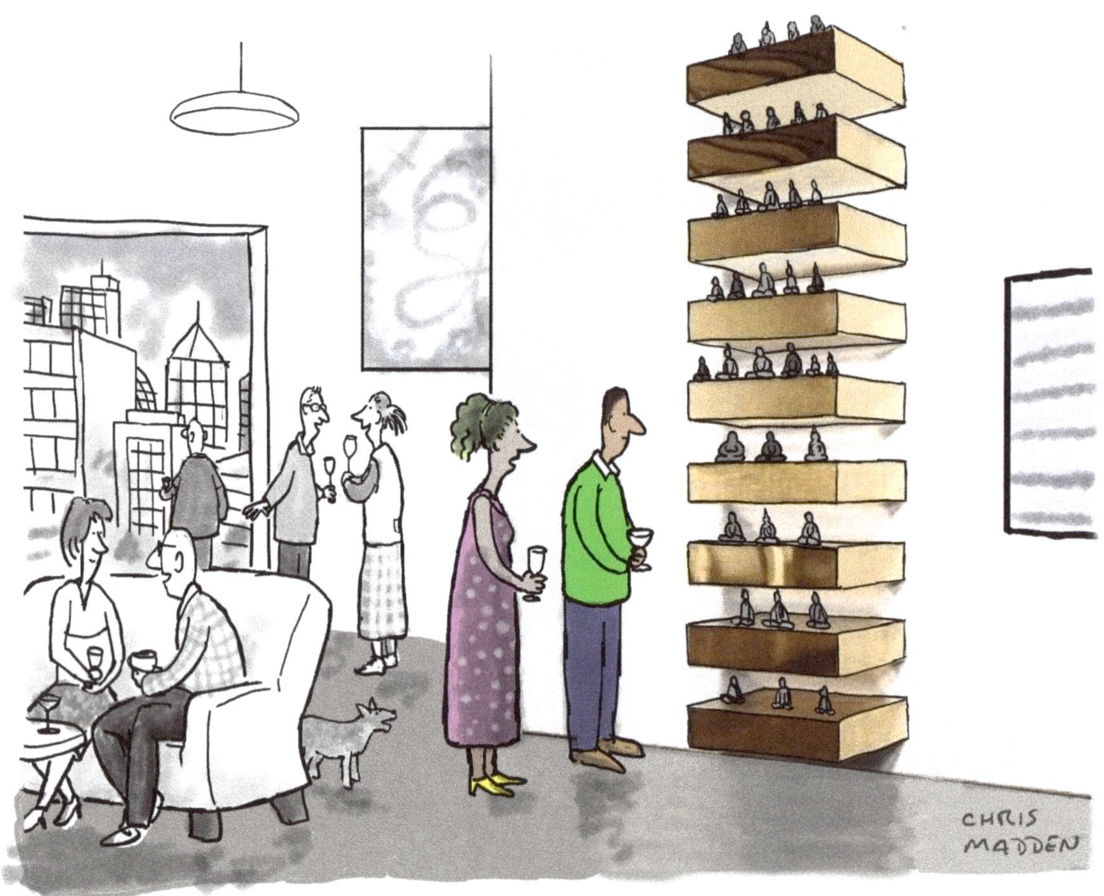

"I'm a huge fan of Donald Judd. My husband's passion is collecting 13th century buddhas."

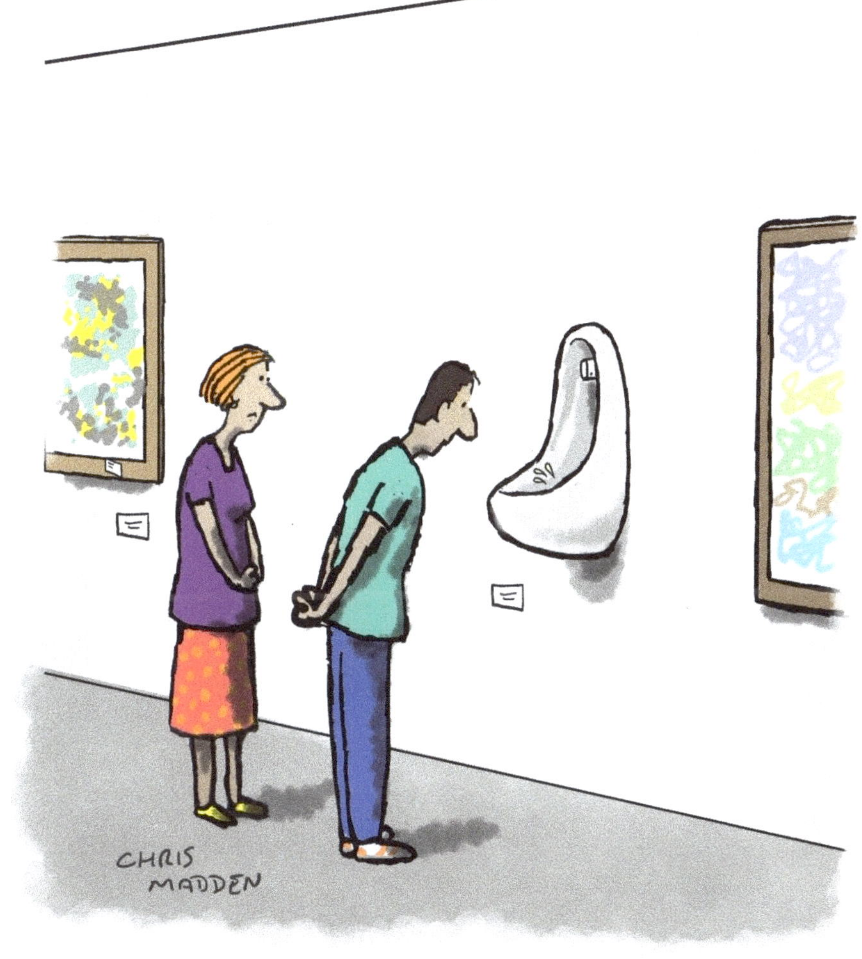

Marcel Duchamp
Drinking Fountain

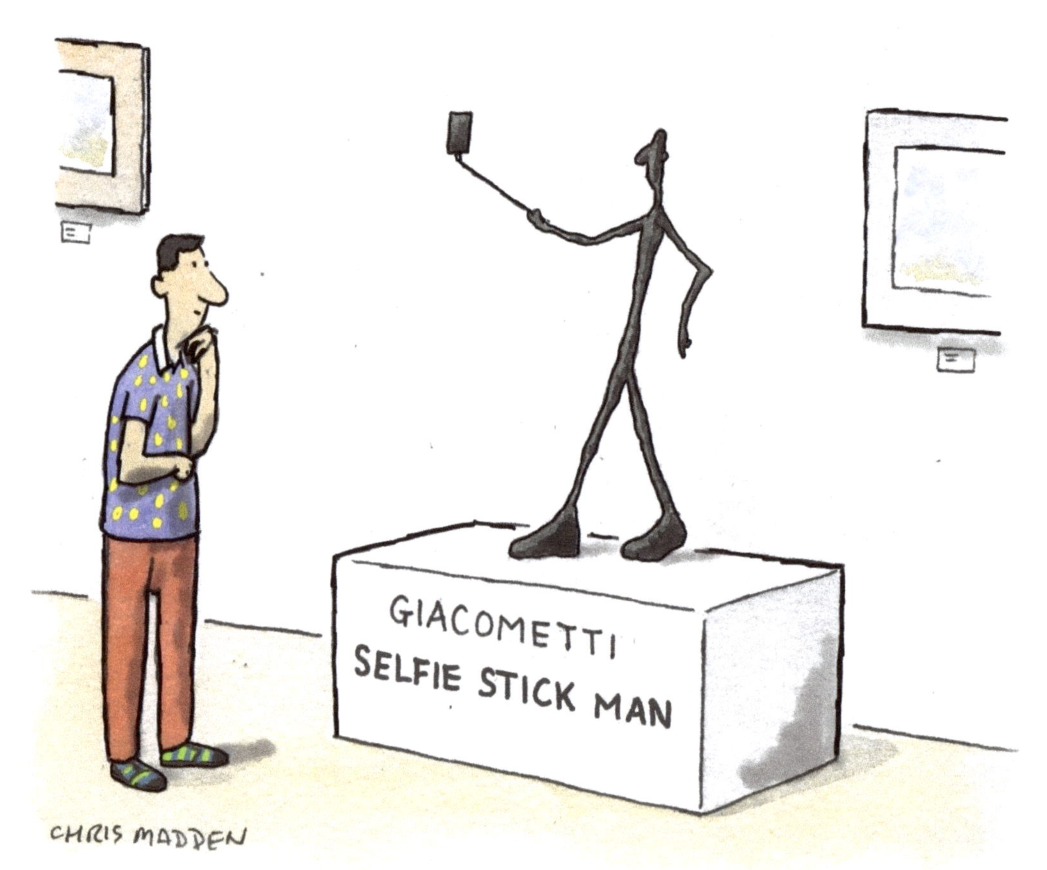
GIACOMETTI
SELFIE STICK MAN
CHRIS MADDEN

NEW DIRECTIONS IN ART

Genetic sculpture

Inserting human DNA into inert clay to create hybrid organic-inorganic sculptures

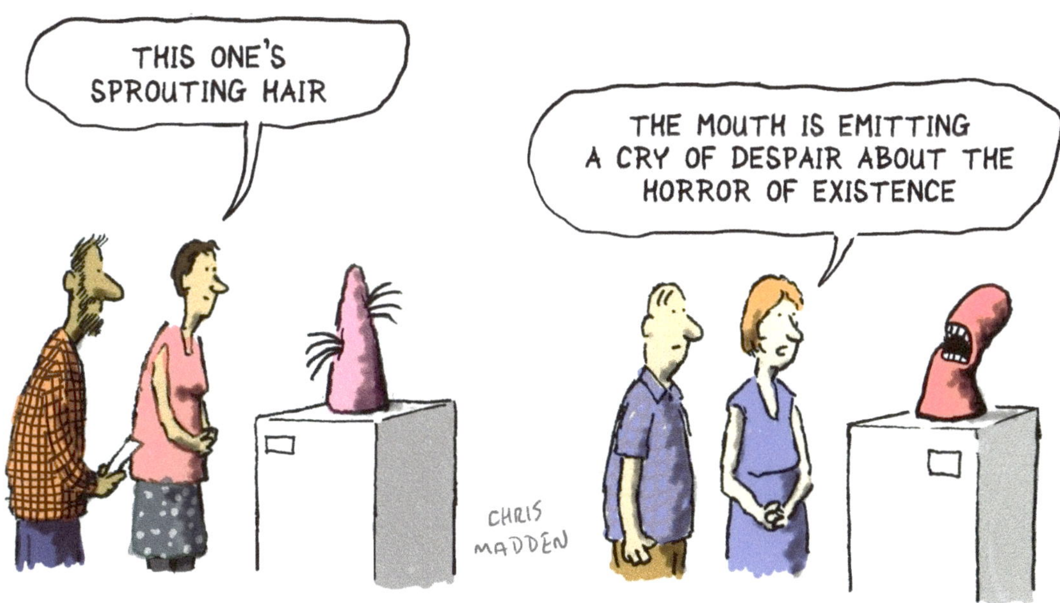

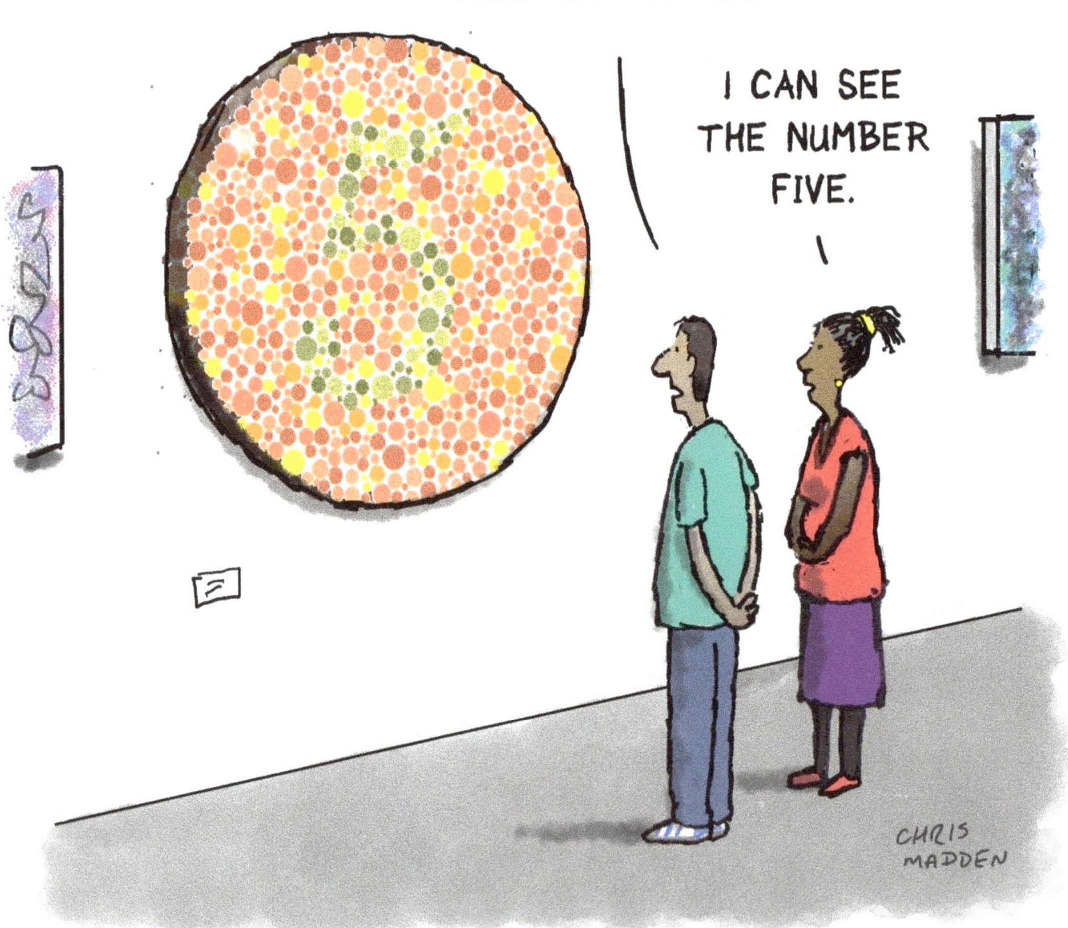
PERSONALLY, I CAN'T SEE ANYTHING IN THIS ONE AT ALL.
I CAN SEE THE NUMBER FIVE.
CHRIS MADDEN

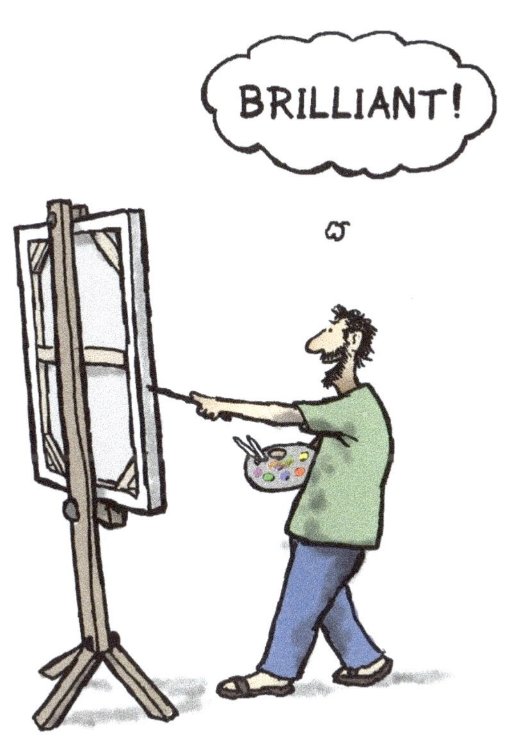

Bad artist

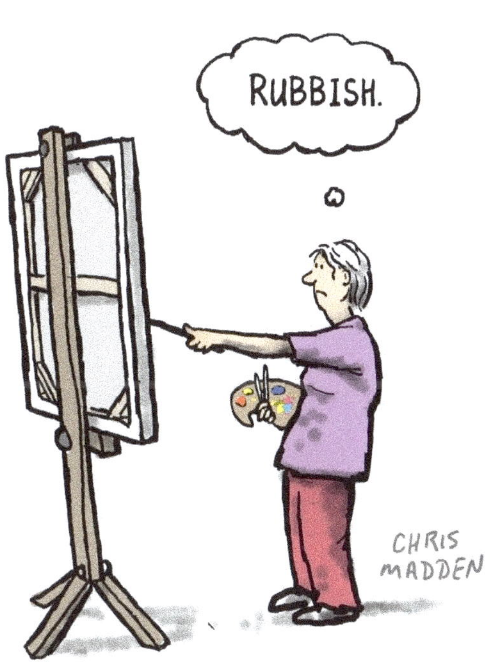

Good artist

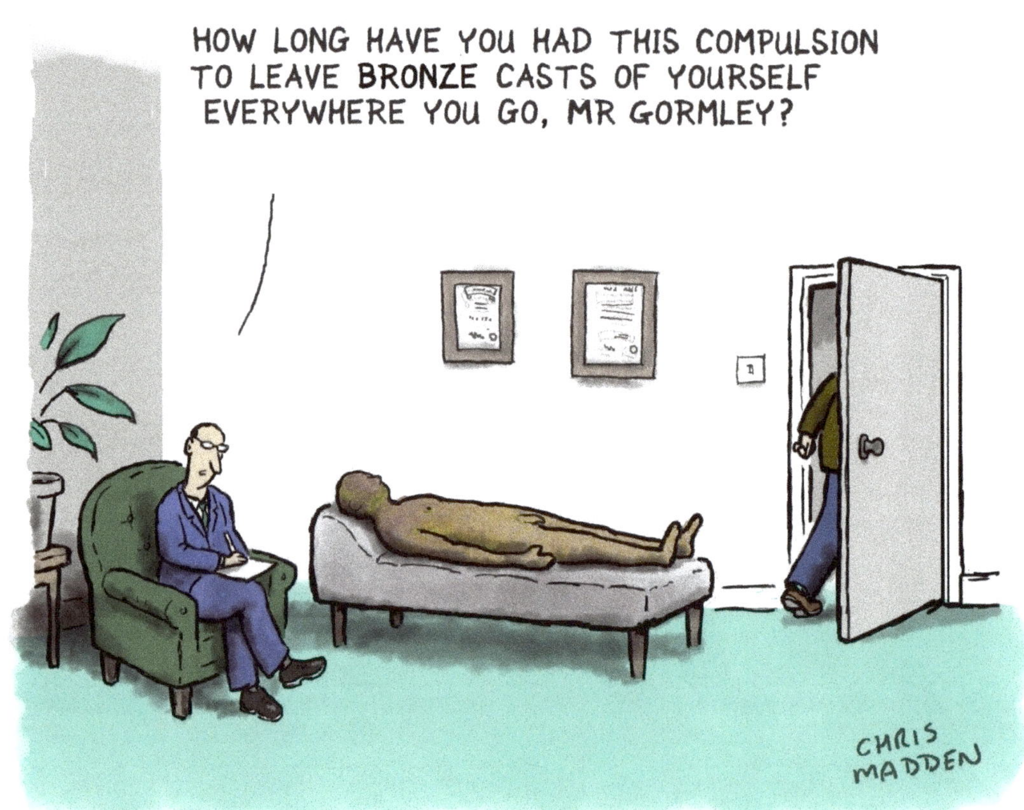
HOW LONG HAVE YOU HAD THIS COMPULSION TO LEAVE BRONZE CASTS OF YOURSELF EVERYWHERE YOU GO, MR GORMLEY?
CHRIS MADDEN

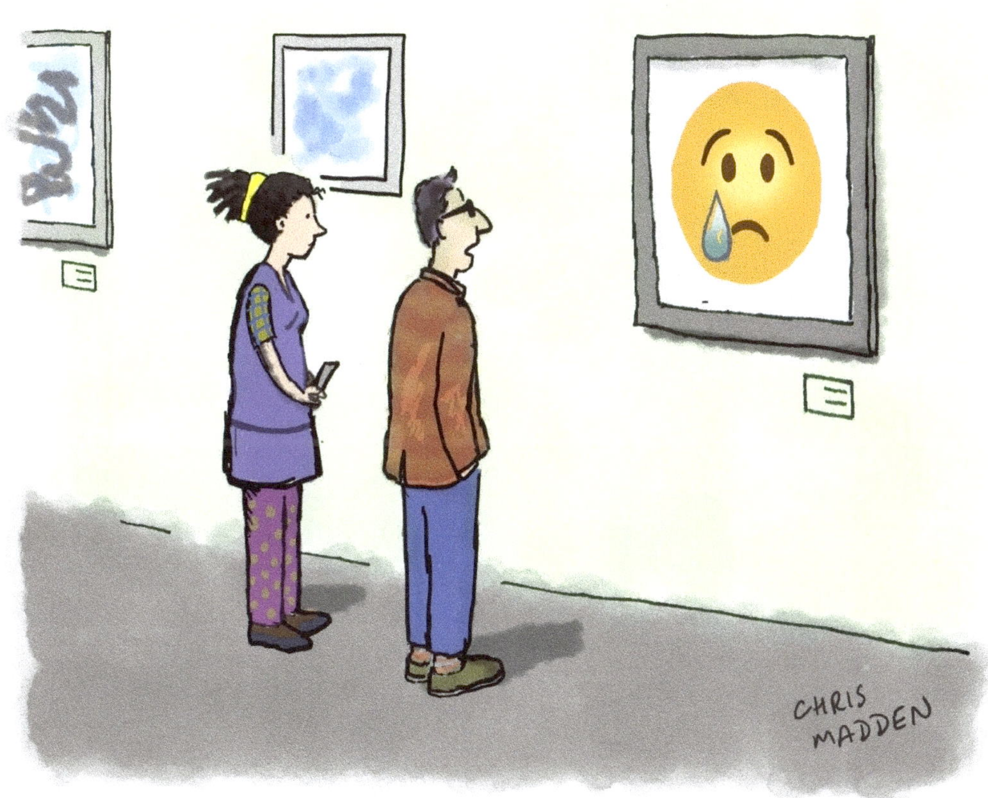

“She’s captured the emotion perfectly!”

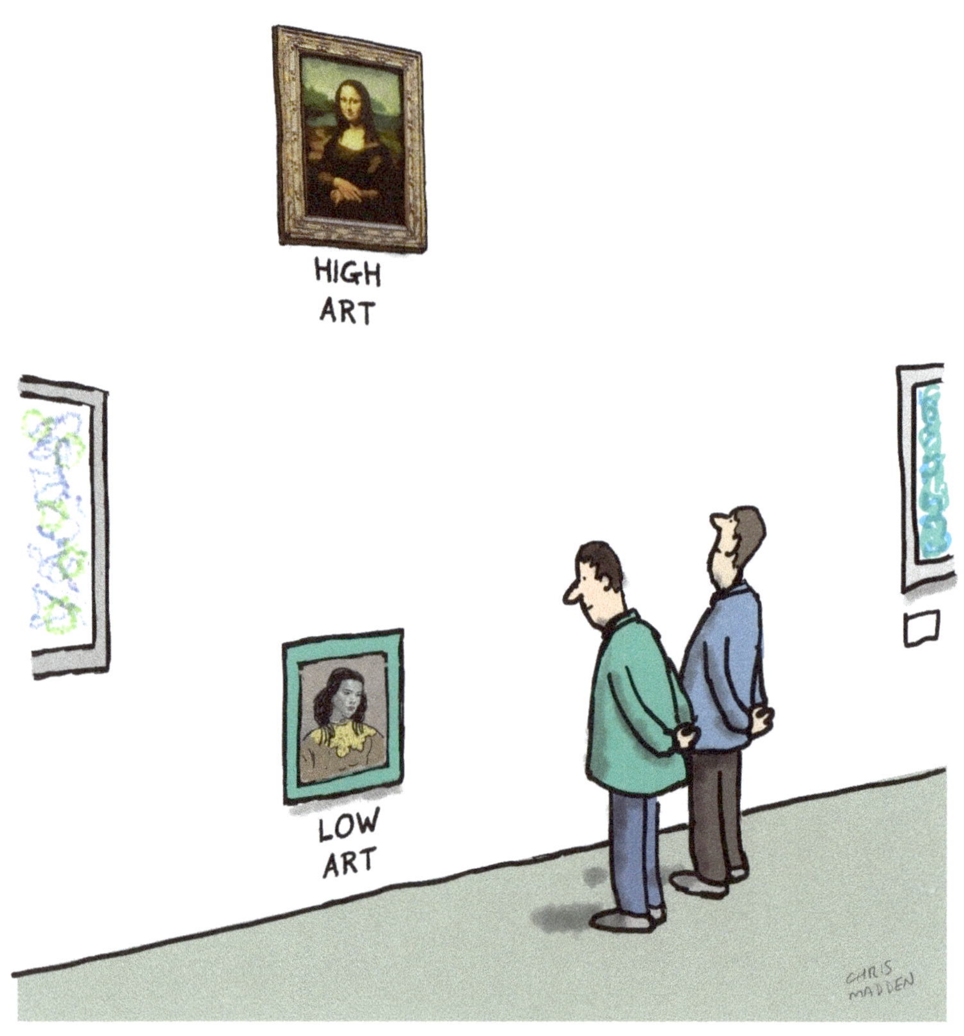
HIGH
ART
LOW
ART
CHRIS
MADDEN

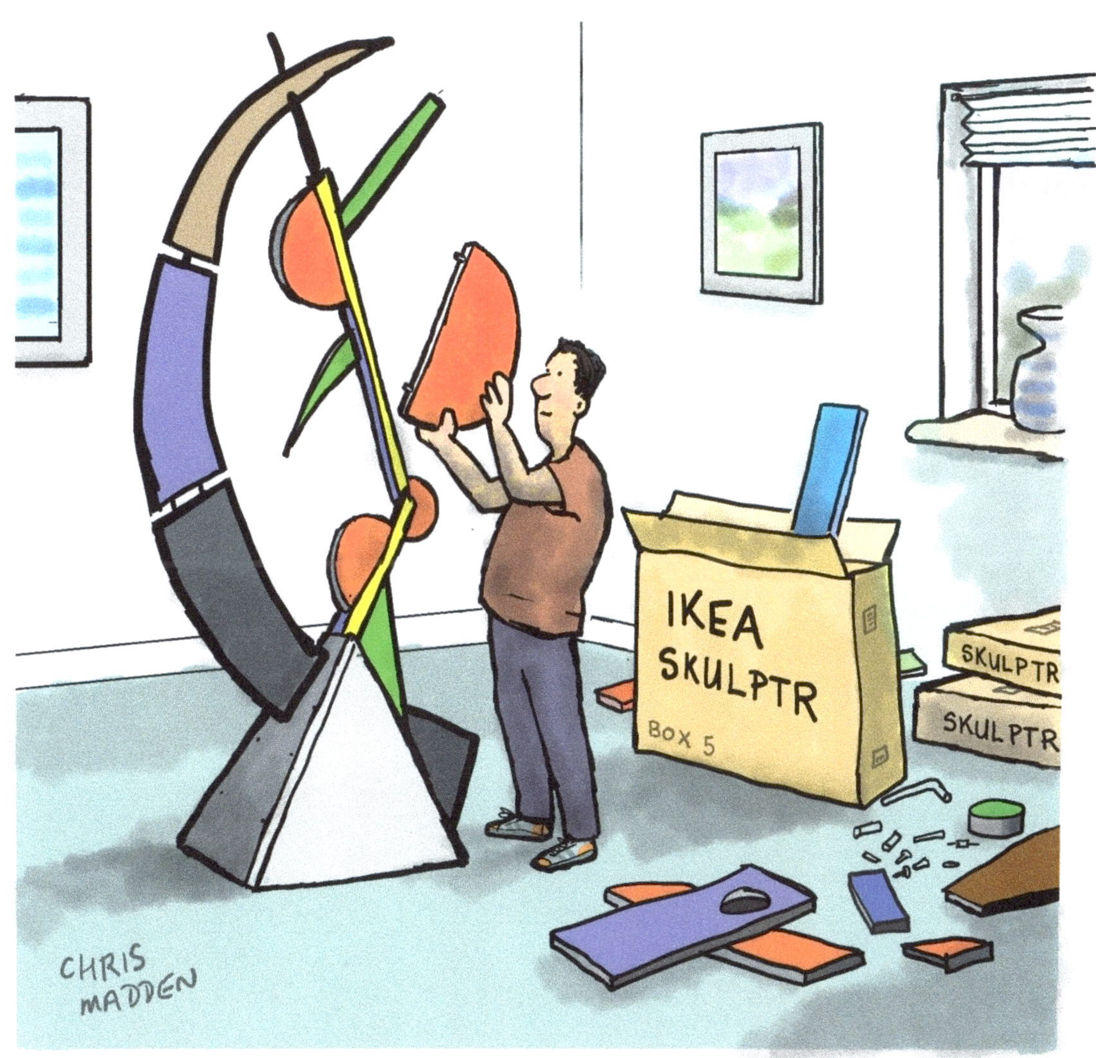
IKEA
SKULPTR
BOX 5
SKULPTR
SKULPTR
CHRIS MADDEN

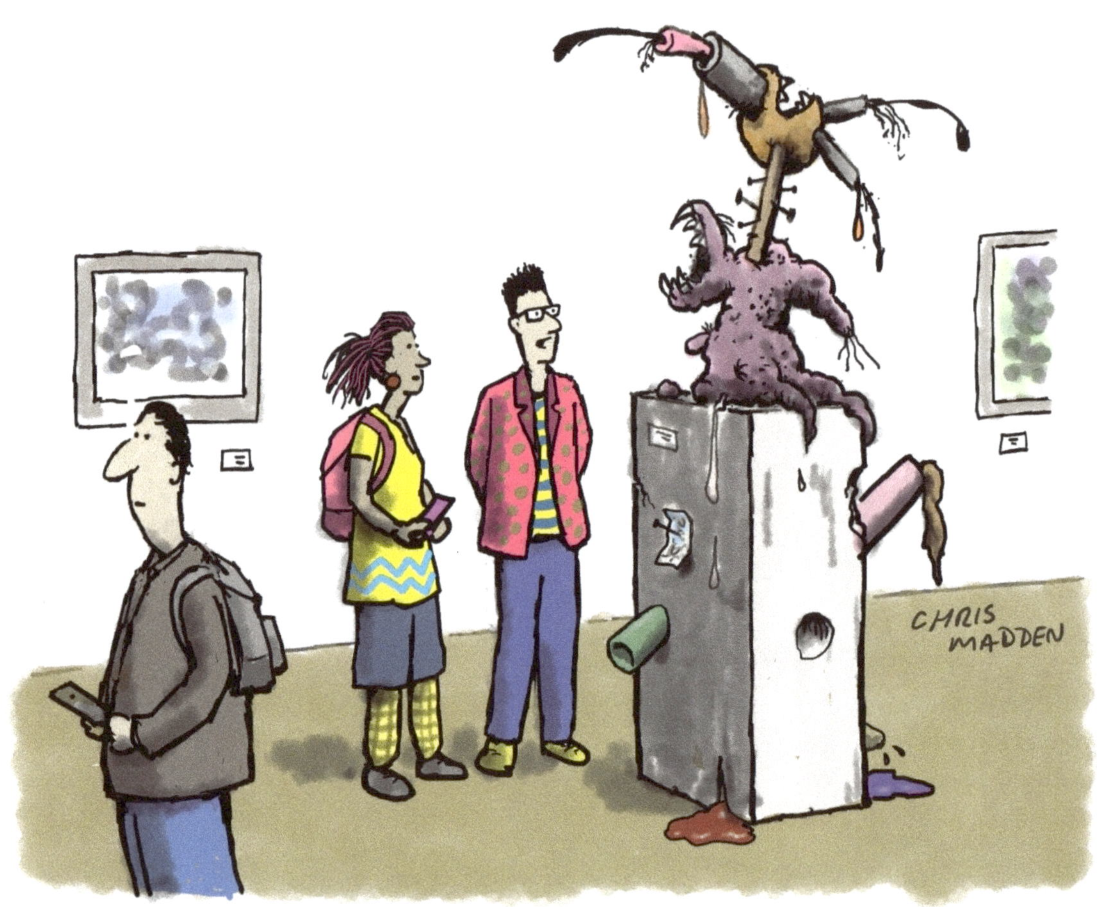

"I like it because of its form and I like it because of its meaning. But most of all I like it because liking it sets me apart from the people who don't like it."

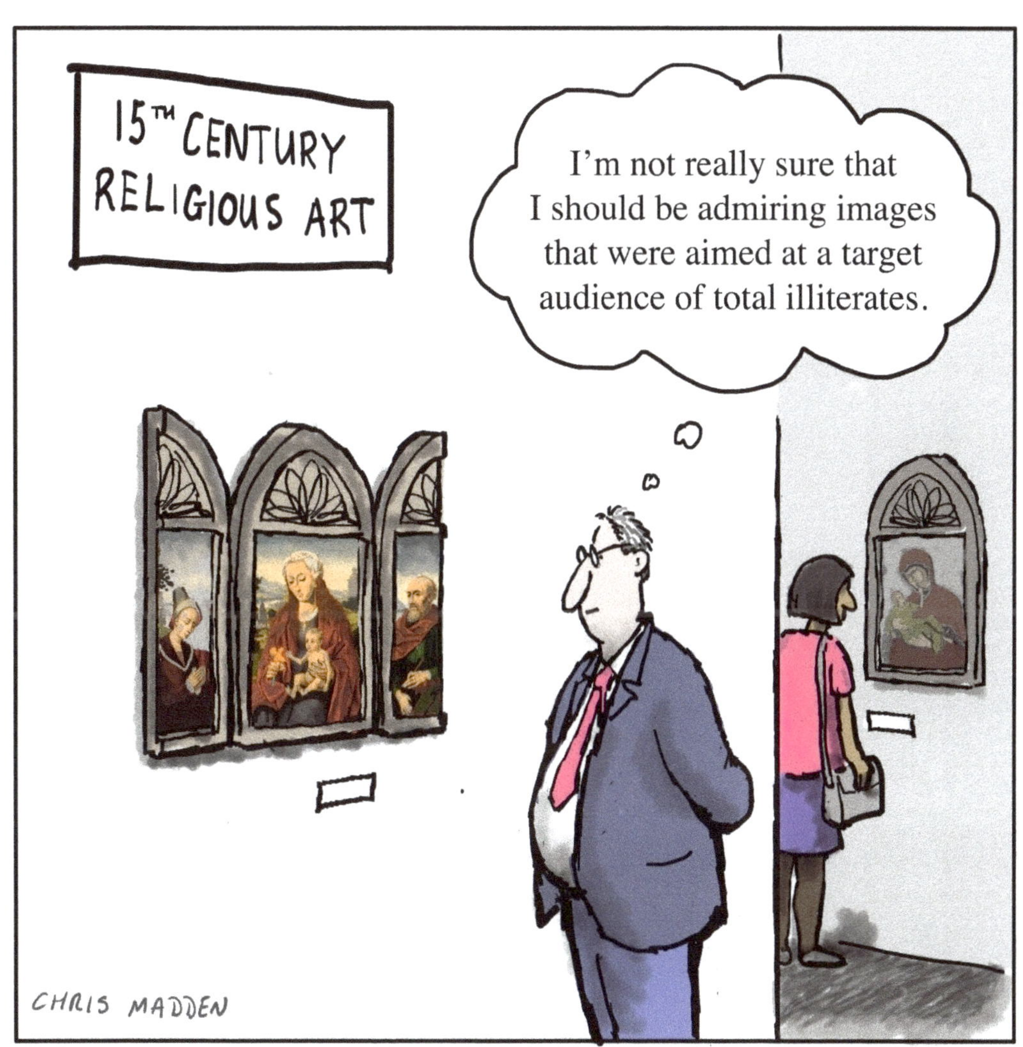
15TH CENTURY RELIGIOUS ART
I'm not really sure that I should be admiring images that were aimed at a target audience of total illiterates.
CHRIS MADDEN

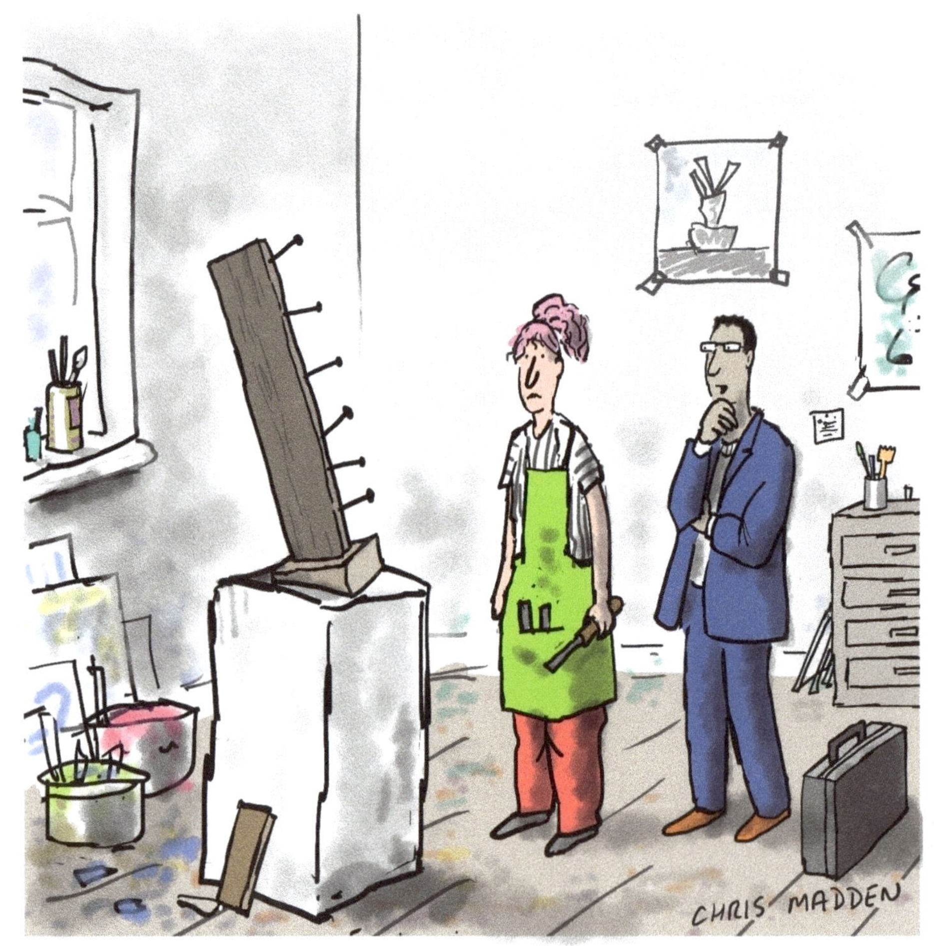

"If we put it on the market for two thousand dollars people will think that it's an over-priced piece of junk. Let's go for ten thousand so they think it's an investment."

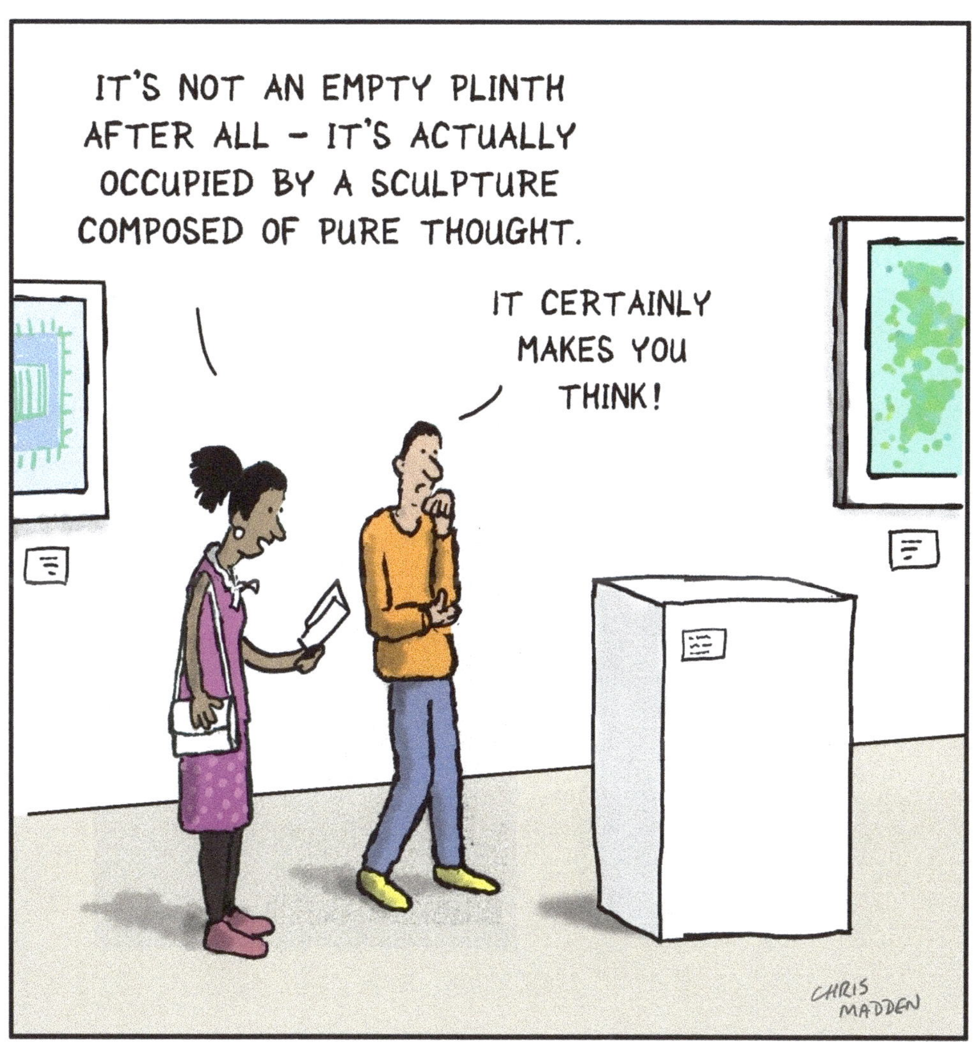
IT'S NOT AN EMPTY PLINTH AFTER ALL – IT'S ACTUALLY OCCUPIED BY A SCULPTURE COMPOSED OF PURE THOUGHT.
IT CERTAINLY MAKES YOU THINK!
CHRIS MADDEN

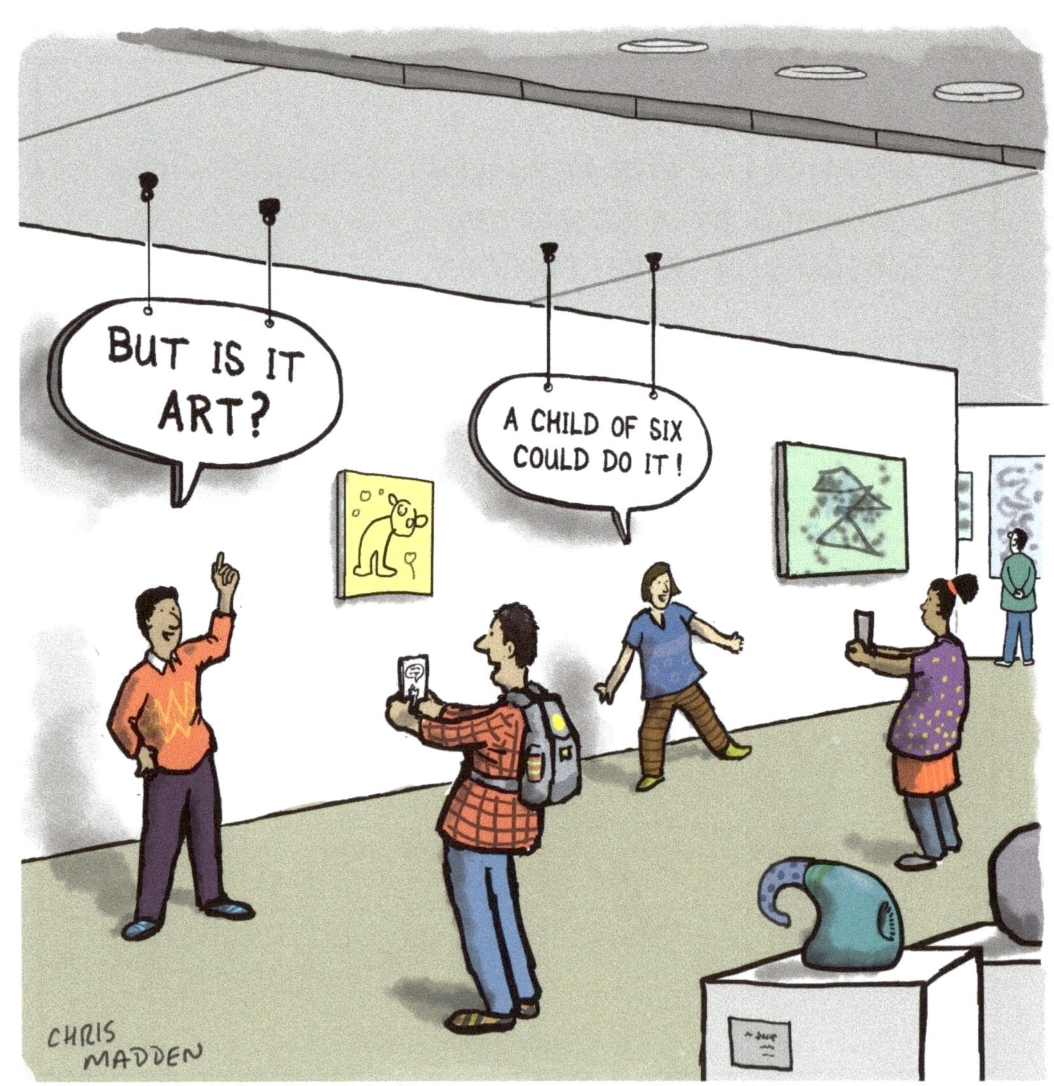
BUT IS IT ART?
A CHILD OF SIX COULD DO IT!
CHRIS MADDEN

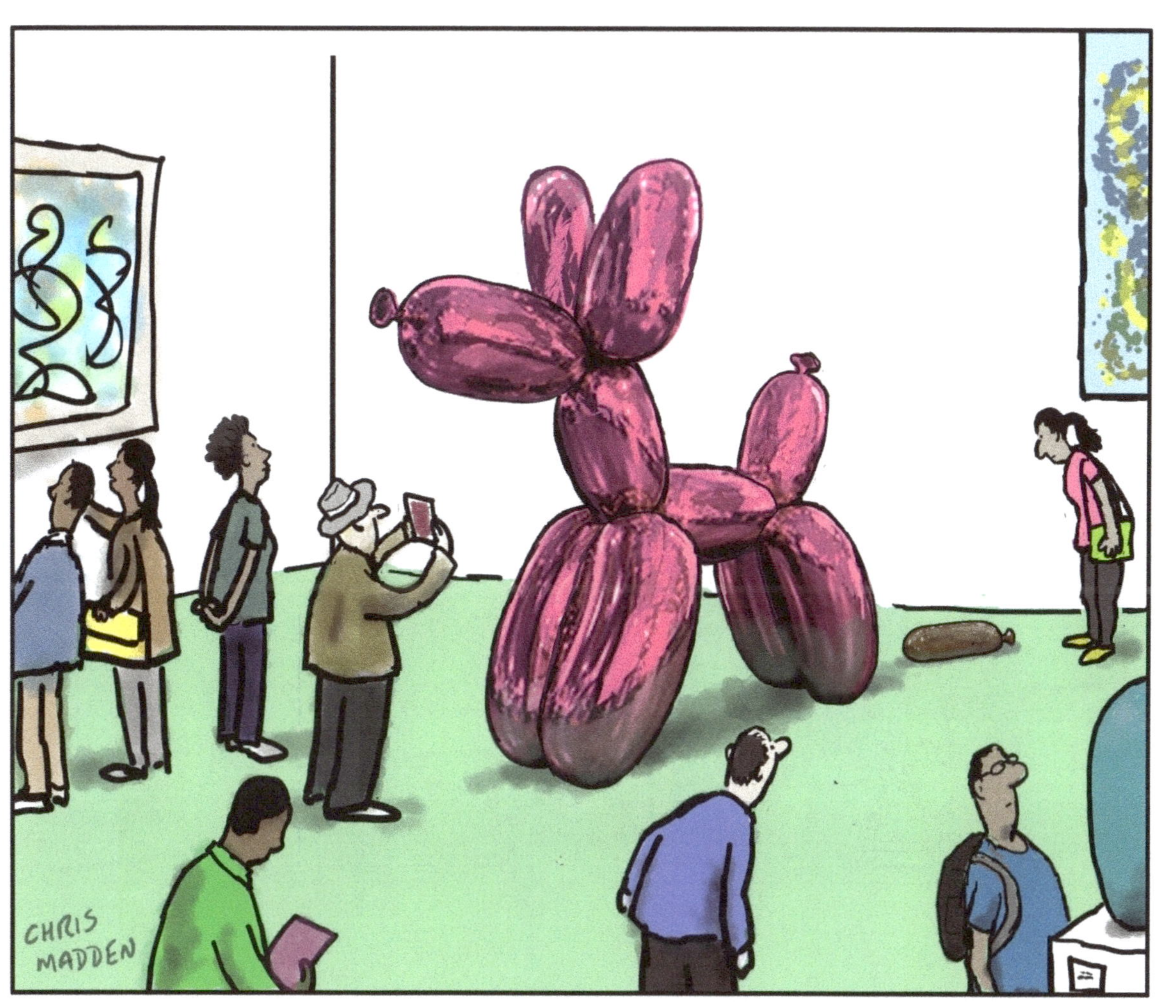
CHRIS
MADDEN

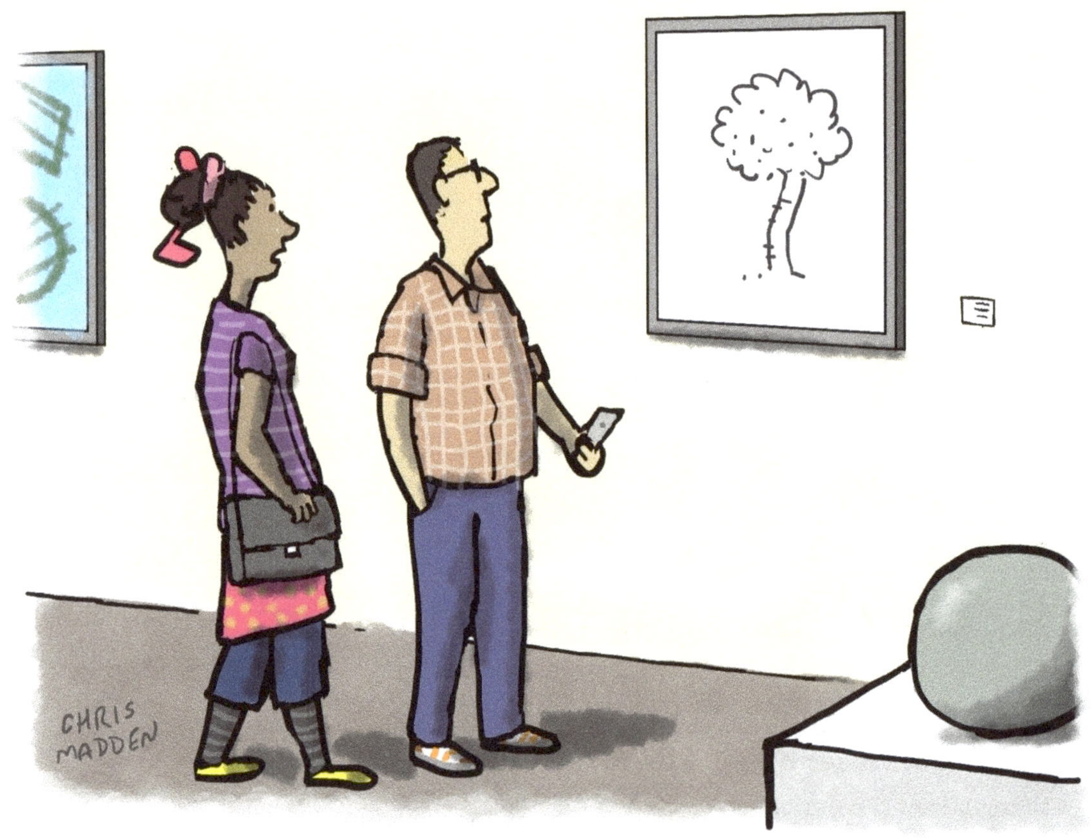

"It's an incredibly meaningful piece of work. The charcoal for the drawing and the paper on which it's drawn were both created from the remains of the very tree that the artist has then depicted, making the work a profound meditation on the nature of death and the purpose of life. The fact that it's a lousy drawing is irrelevant."

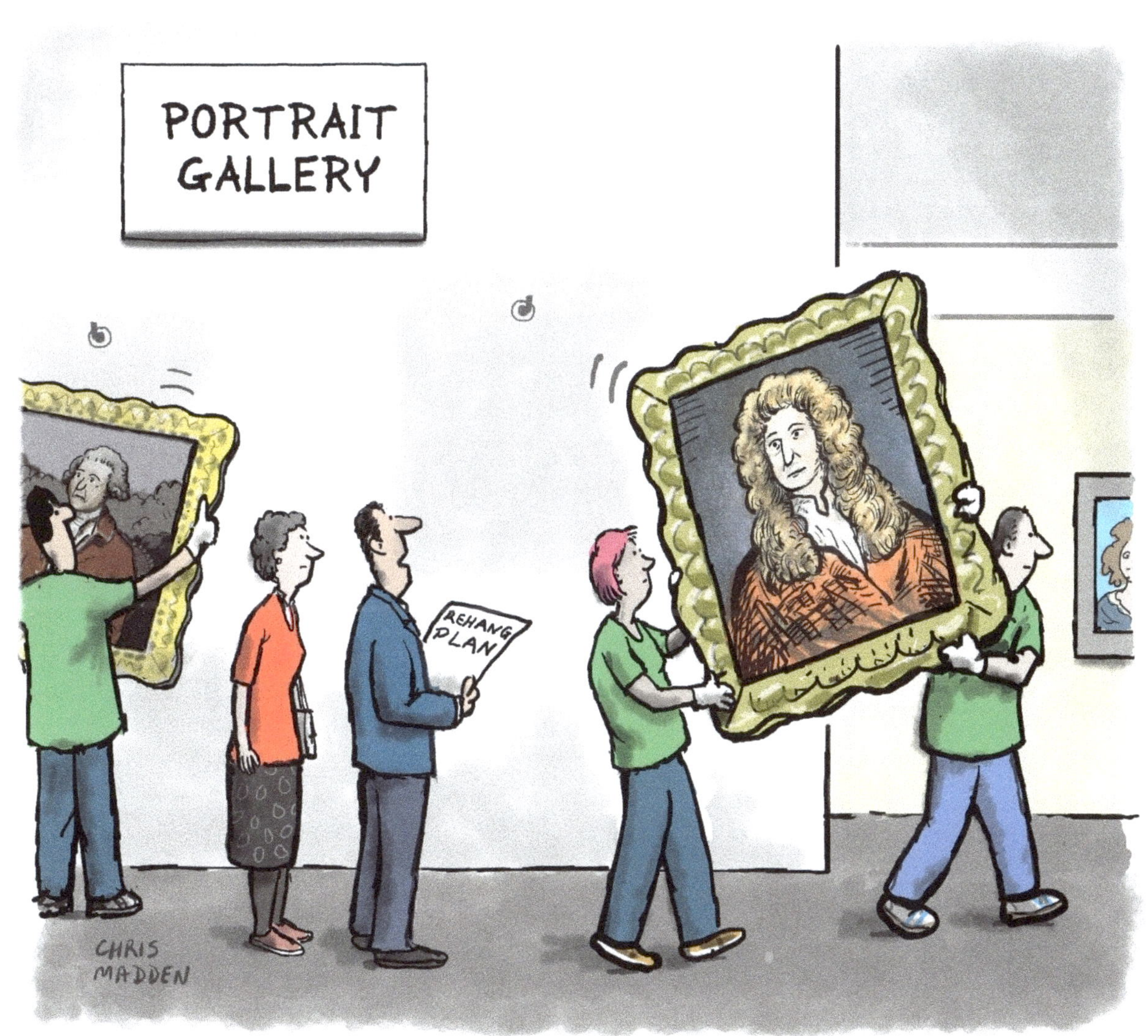

"We're hoping to attract a younger audience by replacing all this old stuff with selfies of social media celebrities."

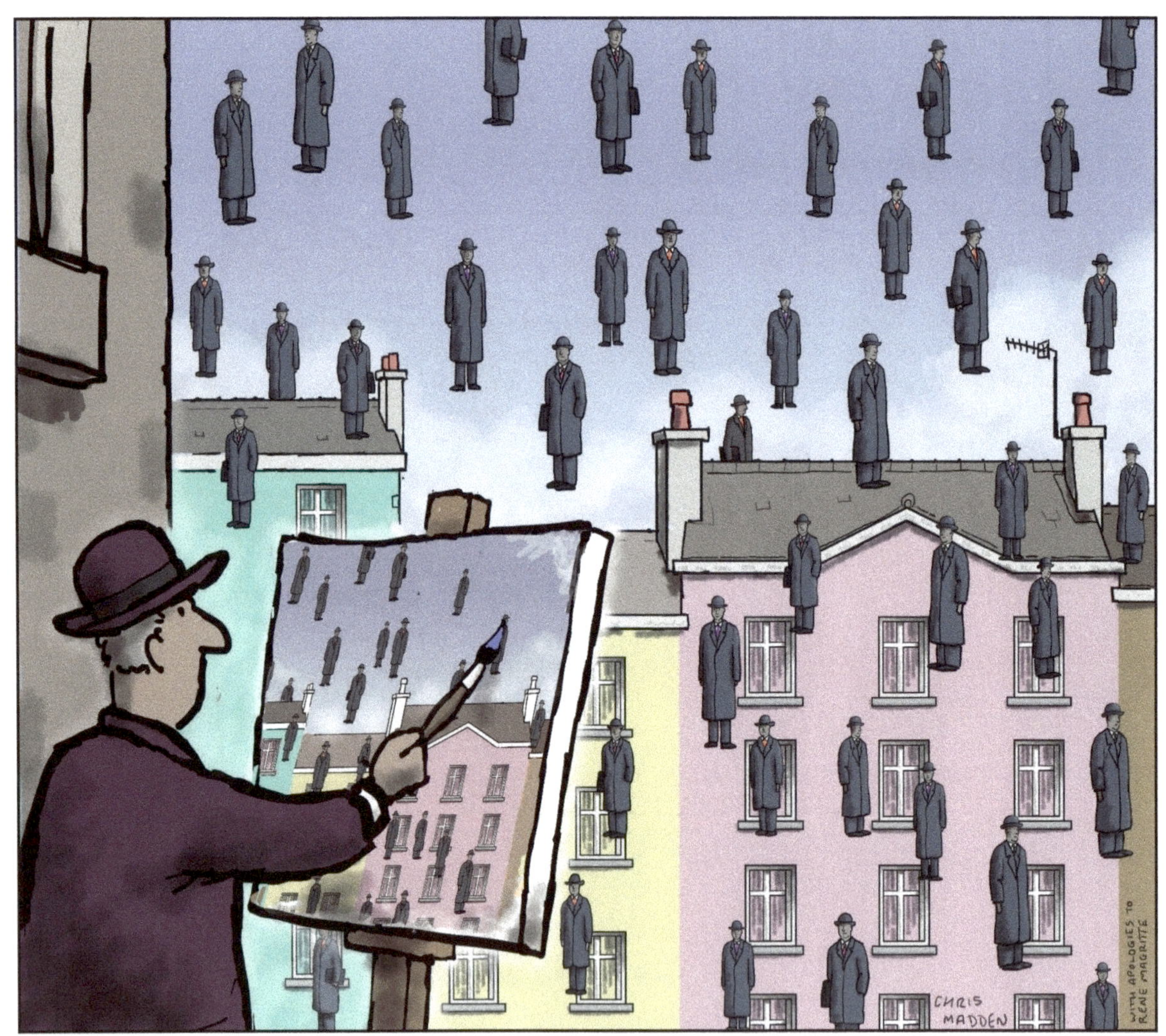
CHRIS MADDEN
WITH APOLOGIES TO RENE MAGRITTE

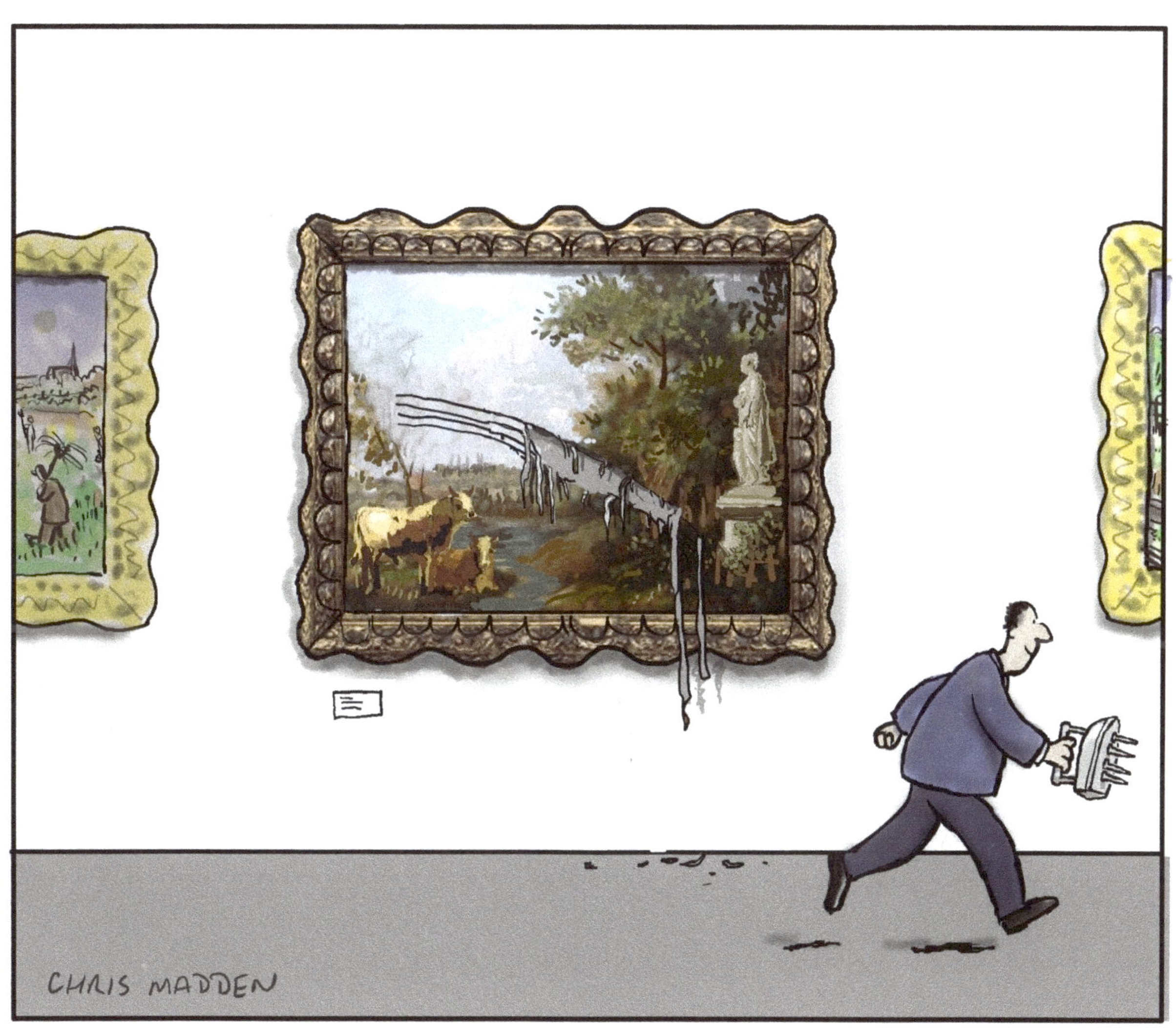

The arrival of modern art

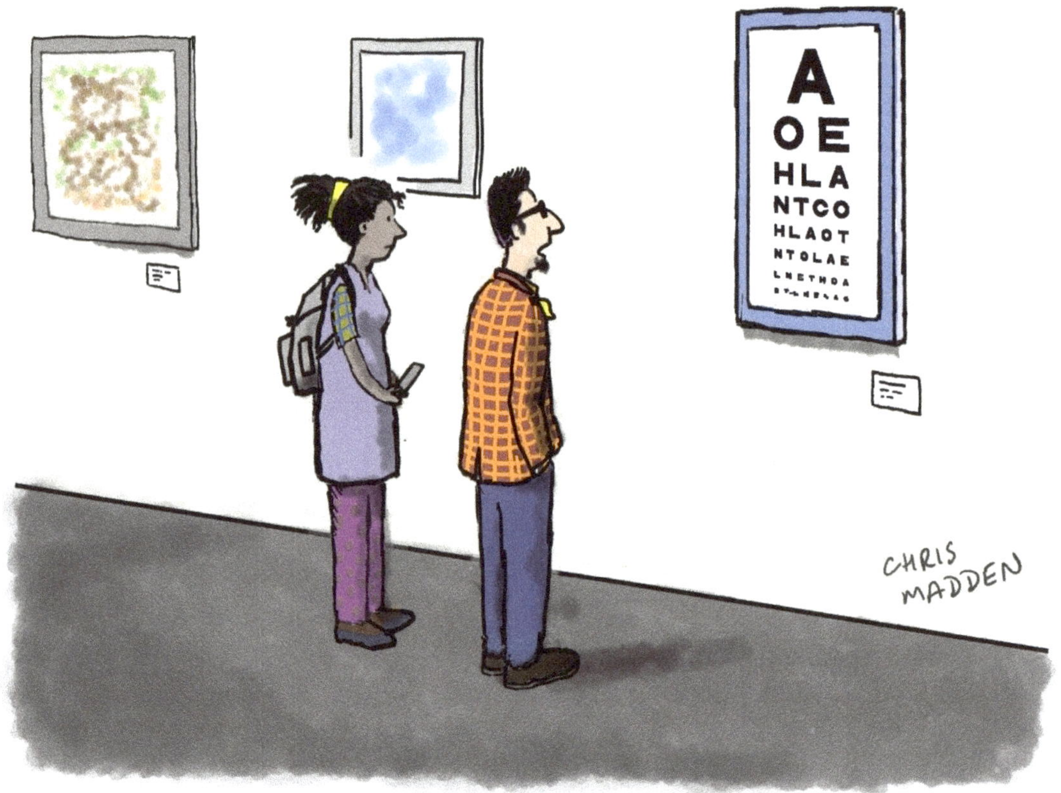

“Yes, I can just about make out what this one’s about – as far as the second line from the bottom that is.”

MODERN ART JIGSAWS

MALEVICH - BLACK SQUARE

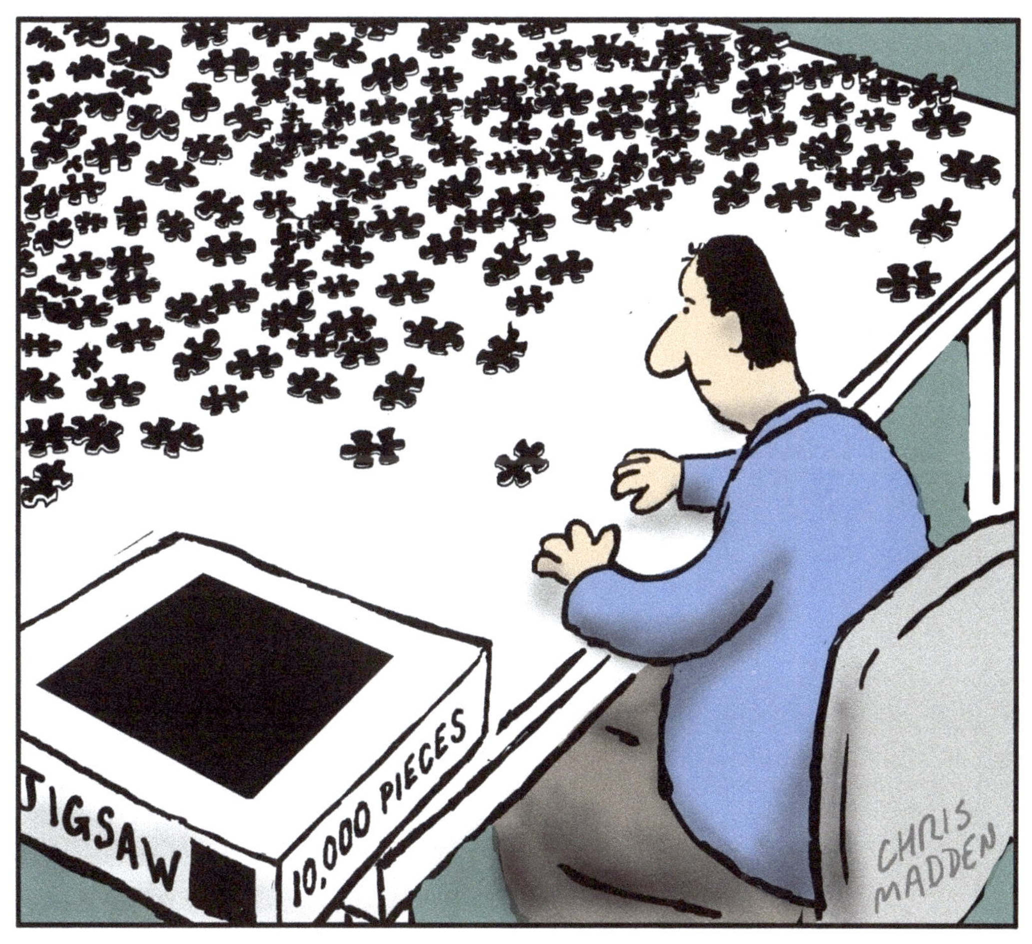

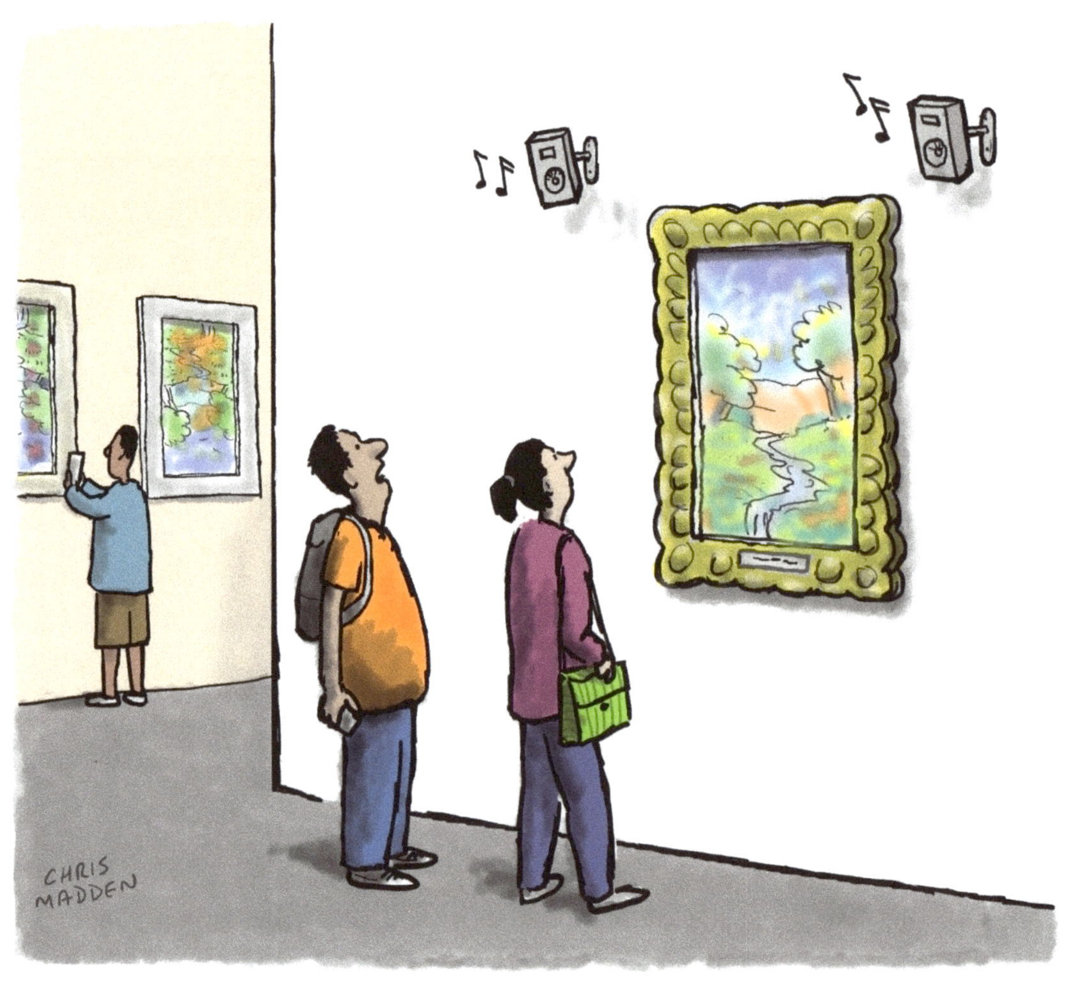

“I’m not keen on this trend for mood music.”

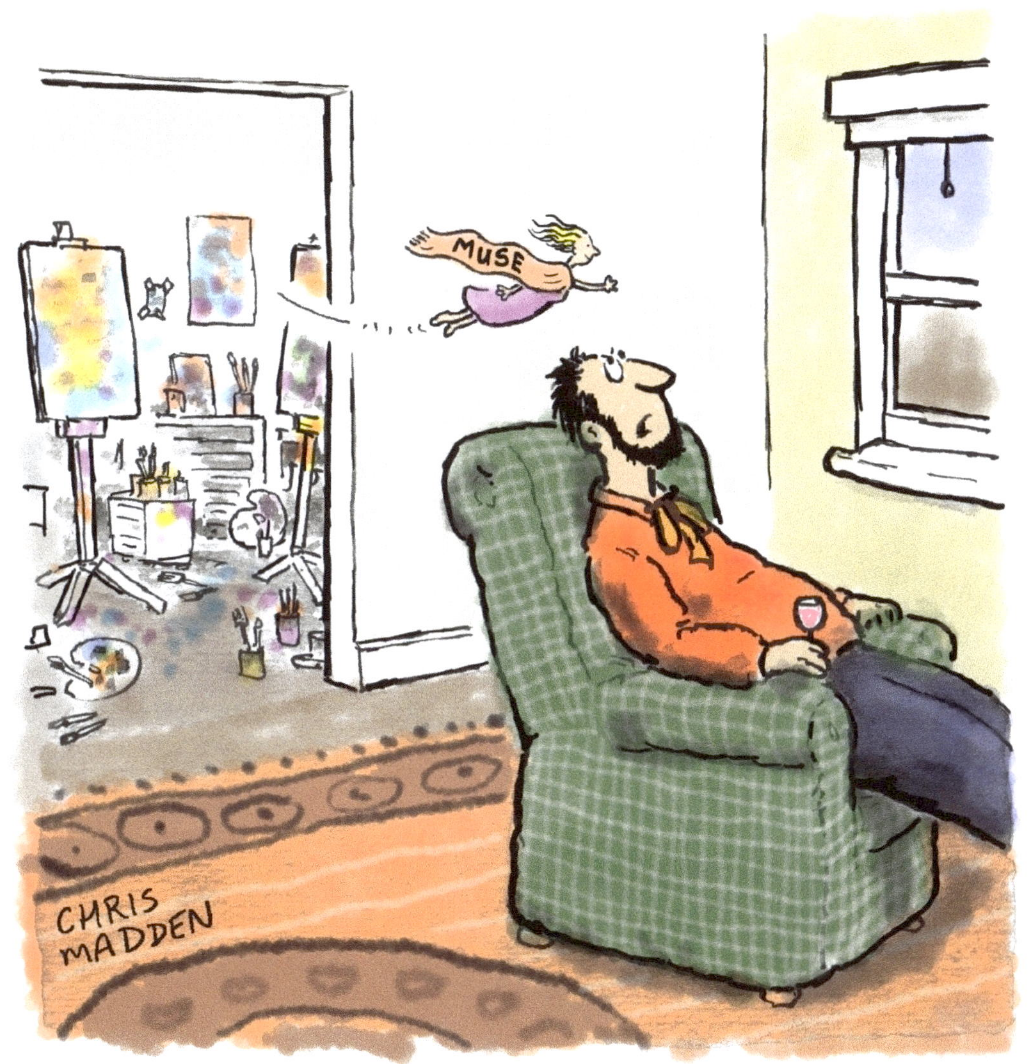

"Go away – I'm trying to relax."

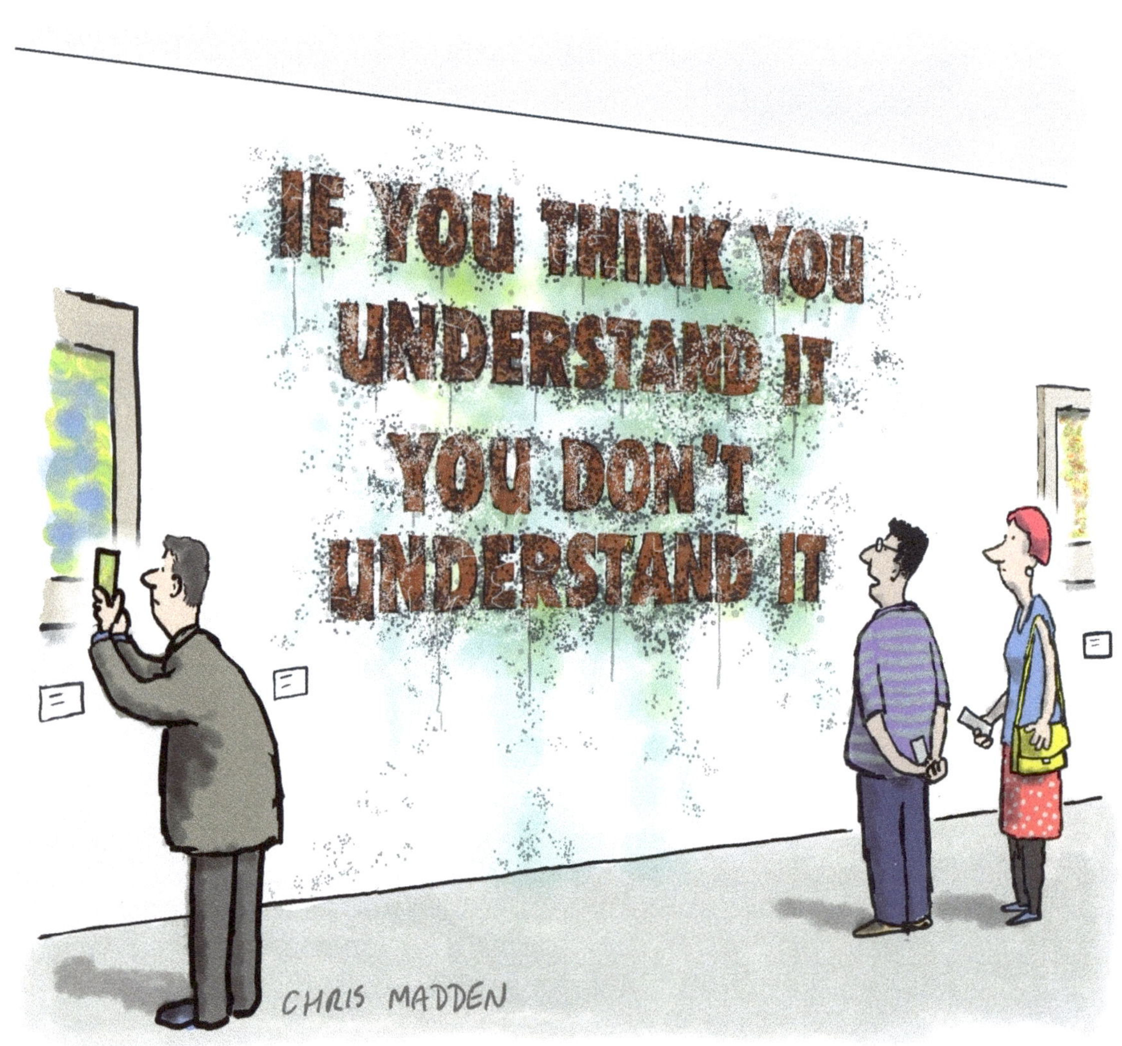

"Of course I understand it!"

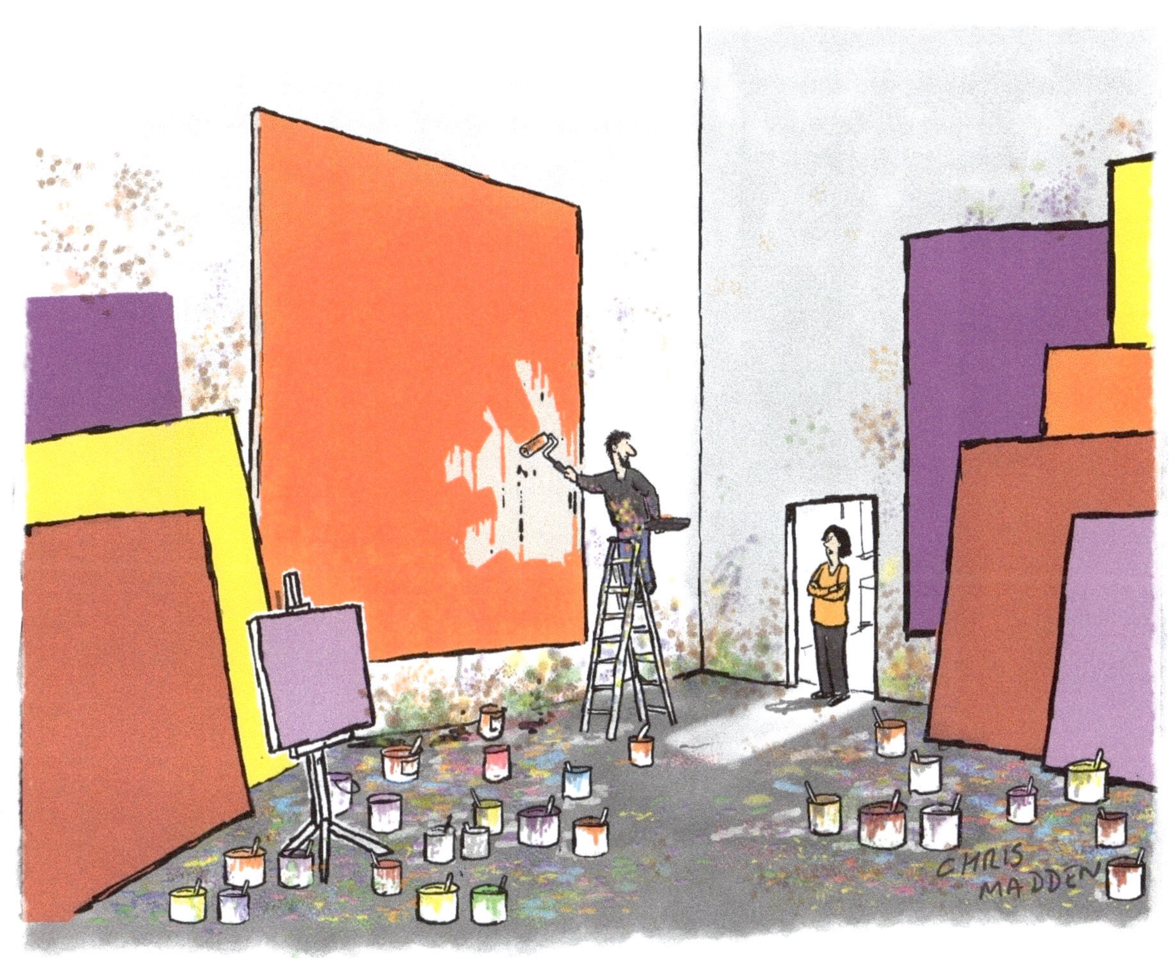

"Maybe after you've finished *'Colour Field 186'*
you could get round to painting the kitchen."

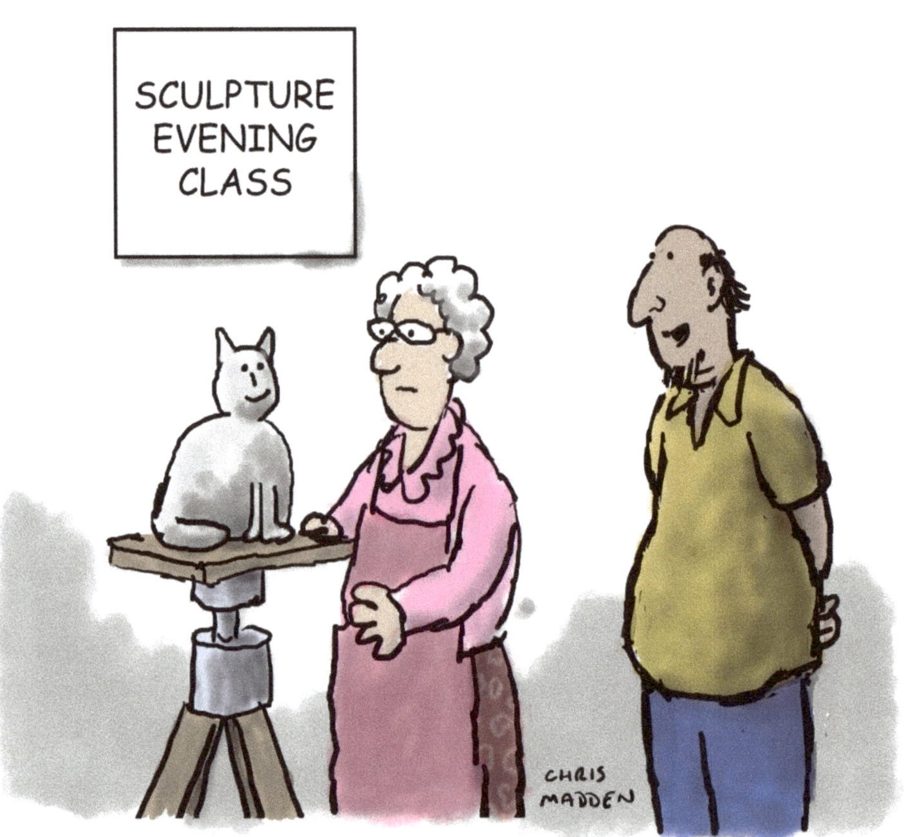

"It's very nice made out of papier-mâché, Doris, but imagine how much more wonderful it would be if it was fashioned from spittle and purifying pig's offal!"

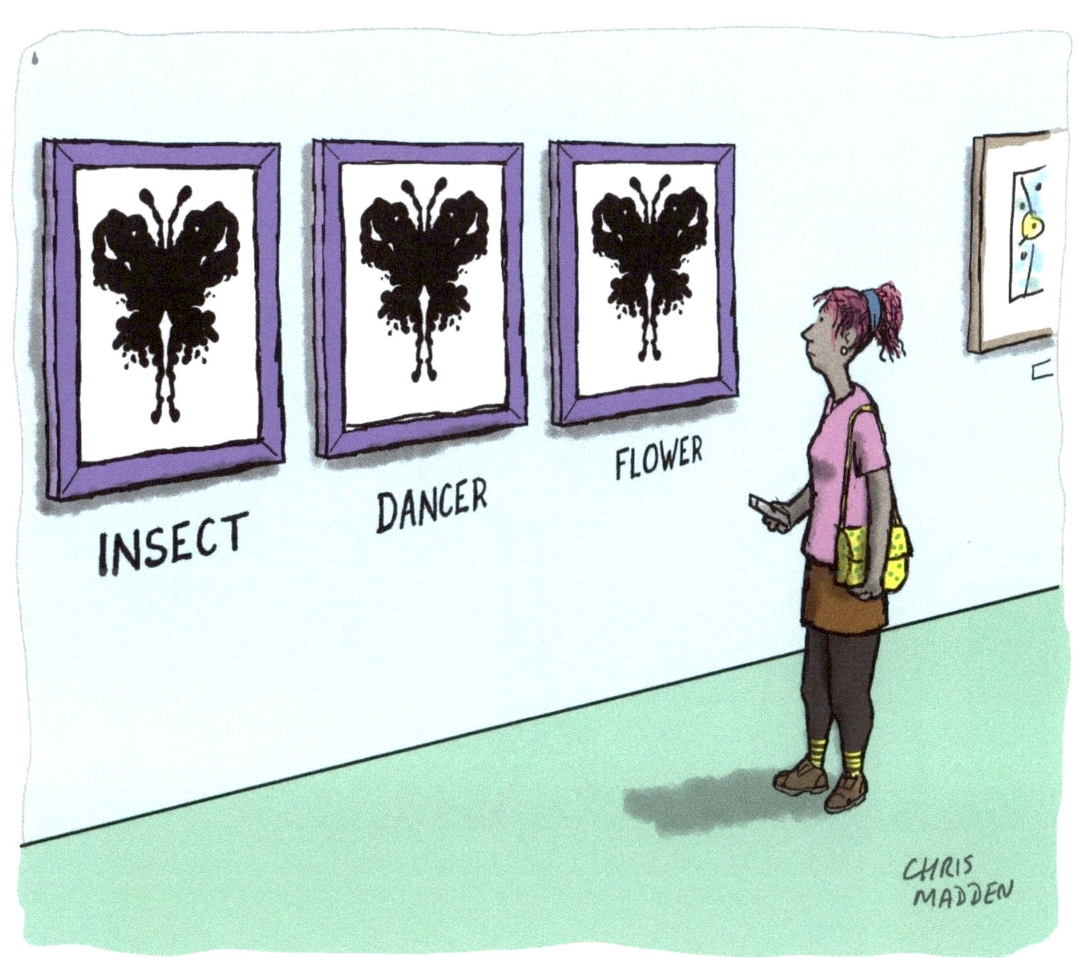
INSECT
DANCER
FLOWER
CHRIS MADDEN

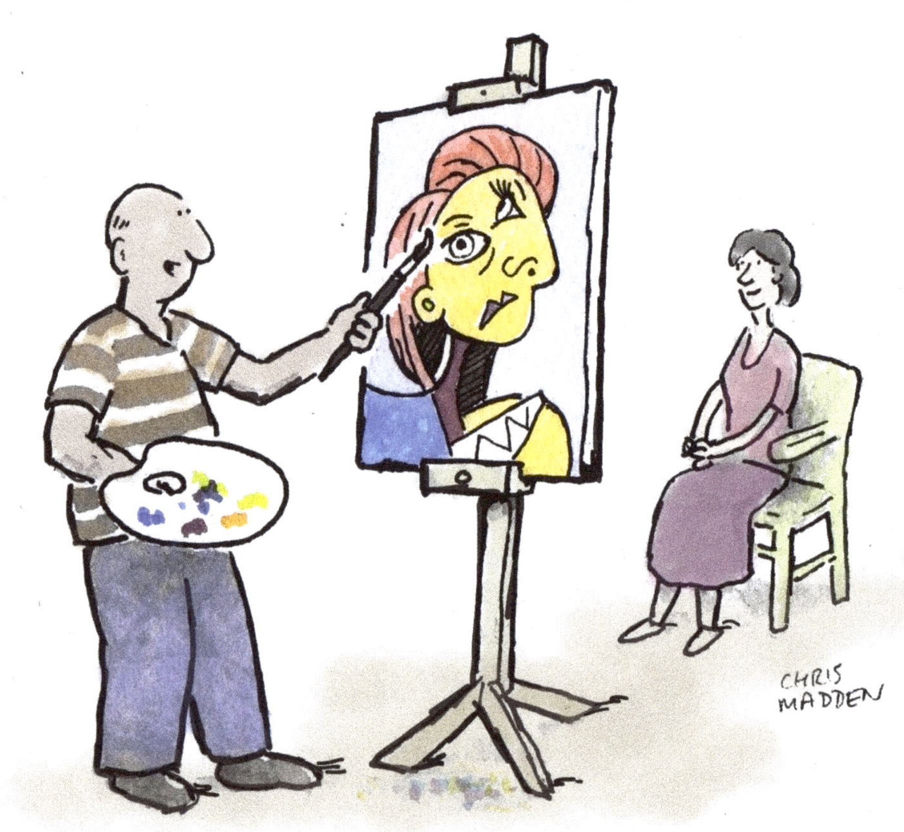

"This painting will make you so famous that you won't be able to walk down the street without being recognised."

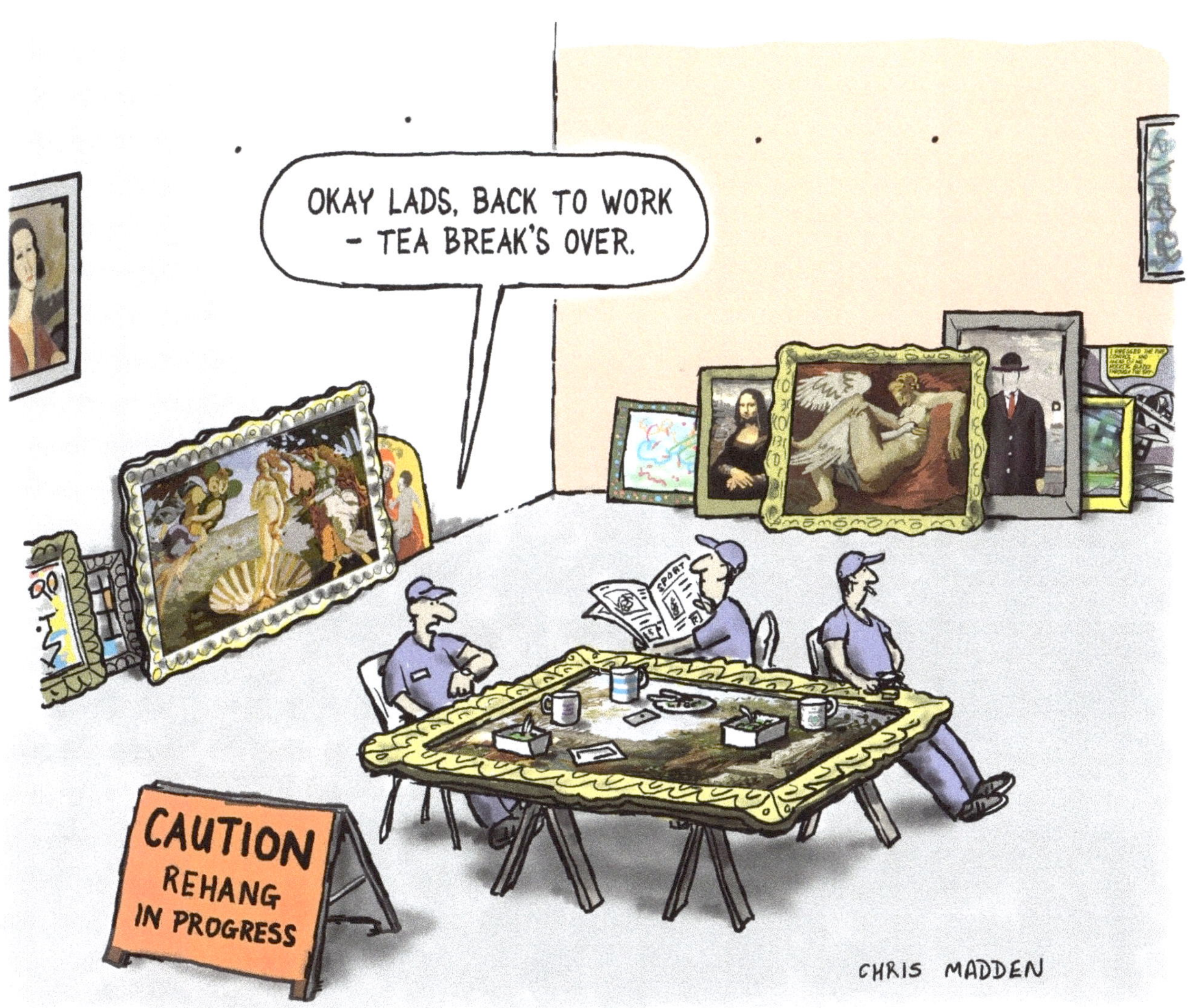
OKAY LADS, BACK TO WORK - TEA BREAK'S OVER.
CAUTION
REHANG
IN PROGRESS
SPORT
CHRIS MADDEN

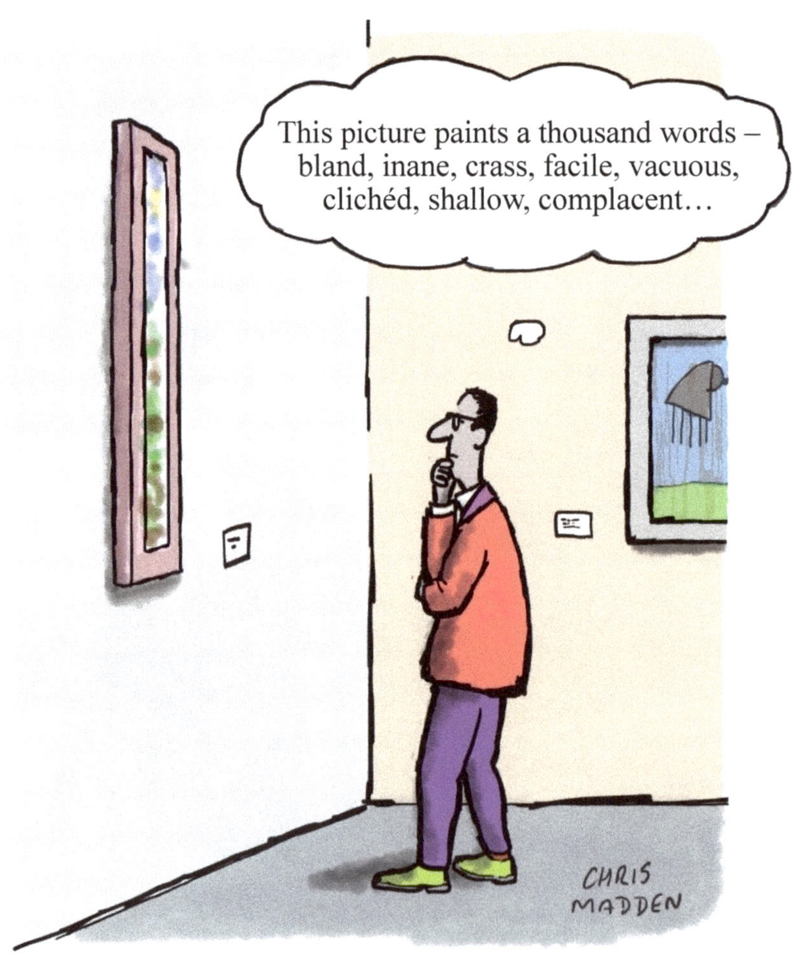
This picture paints a thousand words – bland, inane, crass, facile, vacuous, clichéd, shallow, complacent…
CHRIS MADDEN

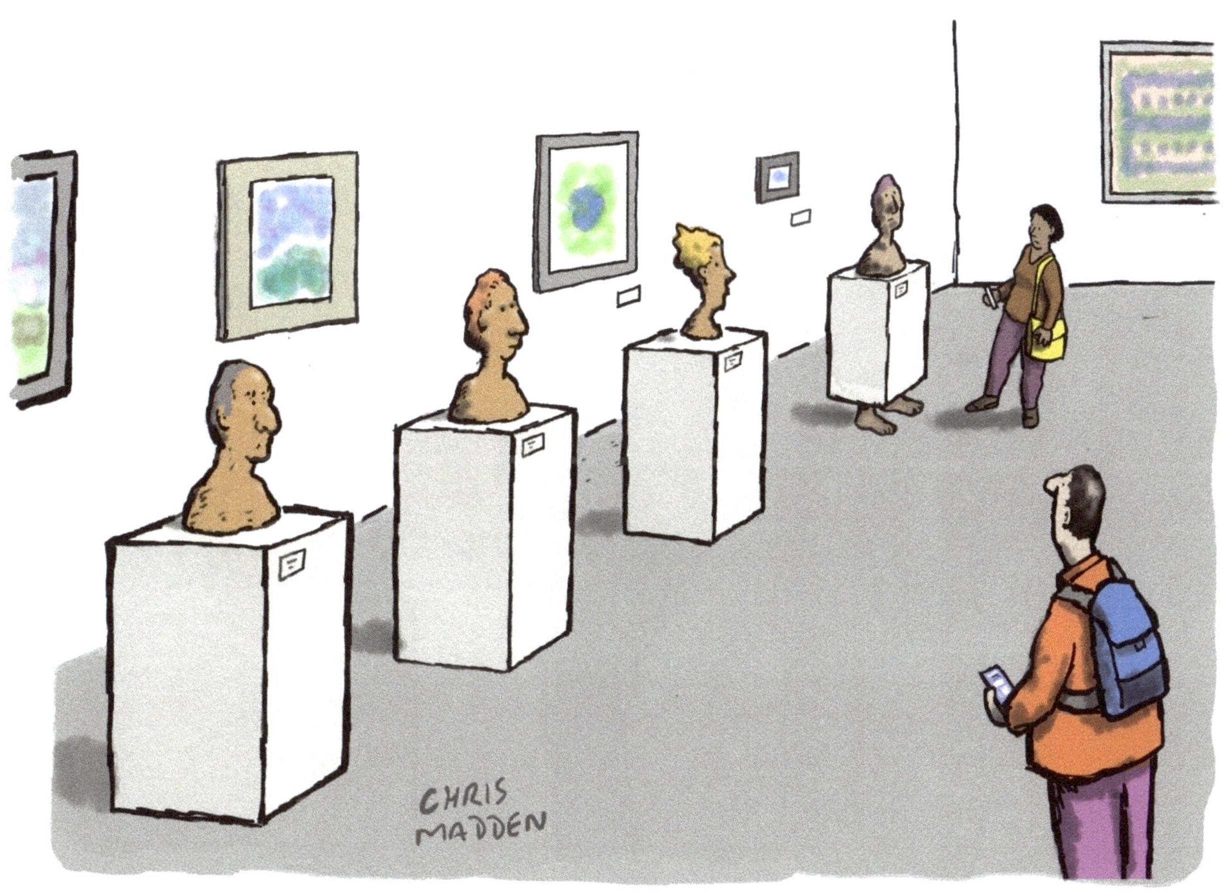
CHRIS
MADDEN

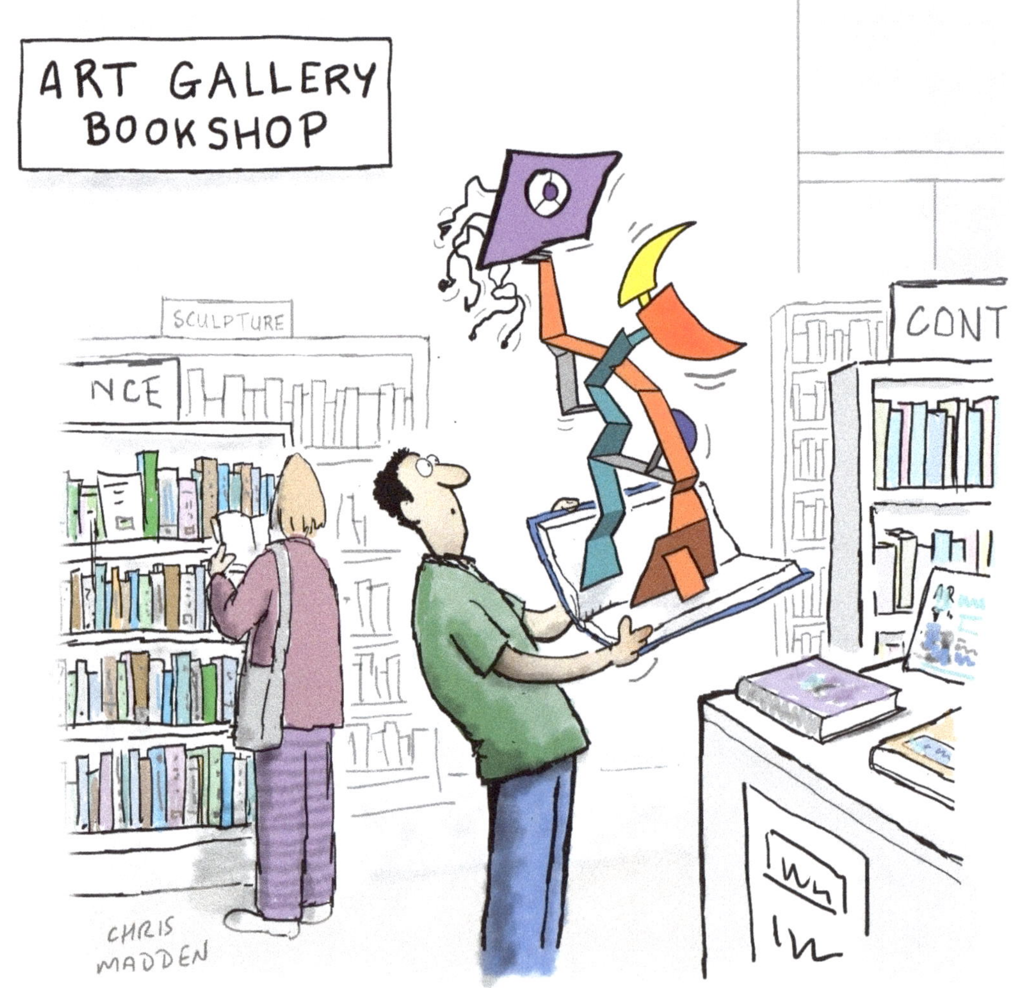

The Pop-up Book of Modern Sculpture

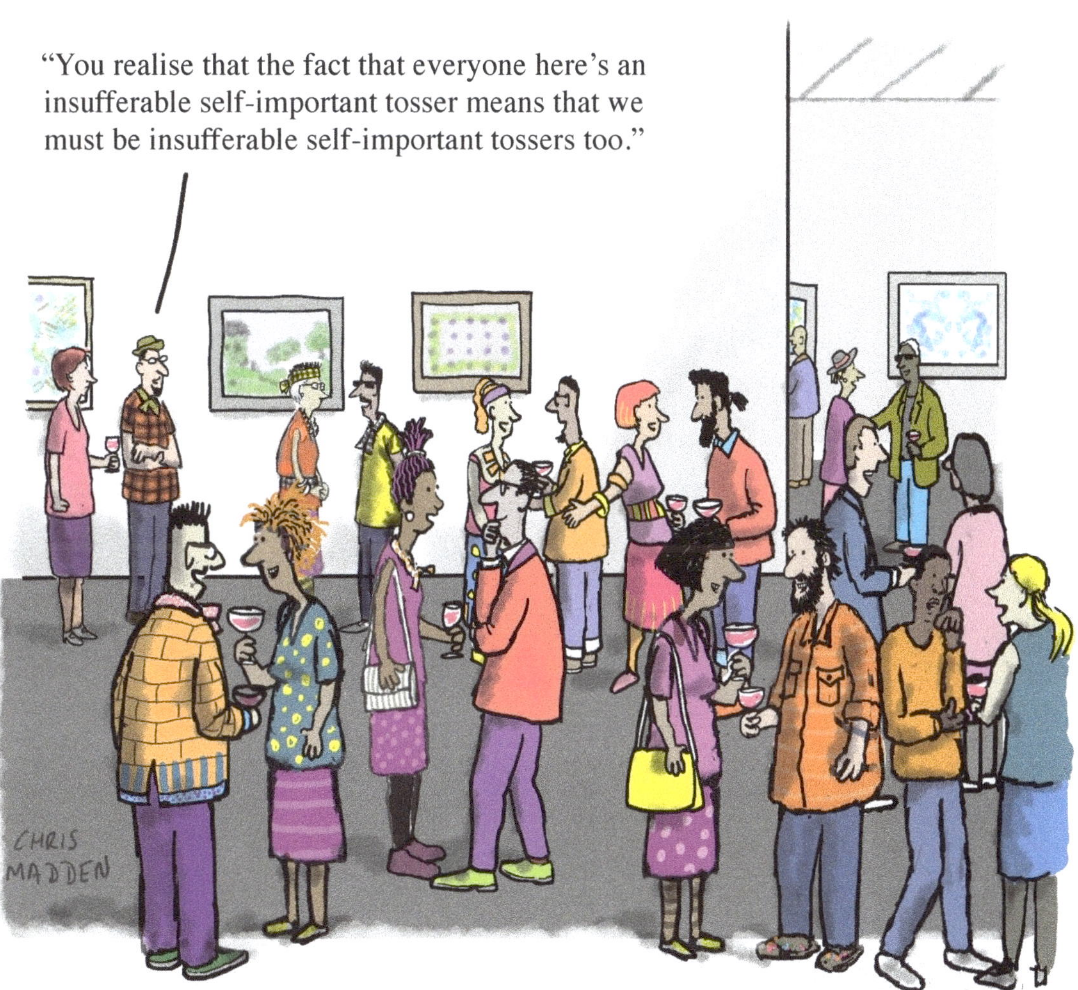
"You realise that the fact that everyone here's an insufferable self-important tosser means that we must be insufferable self-important tossers too."
CHRIS MADDEN

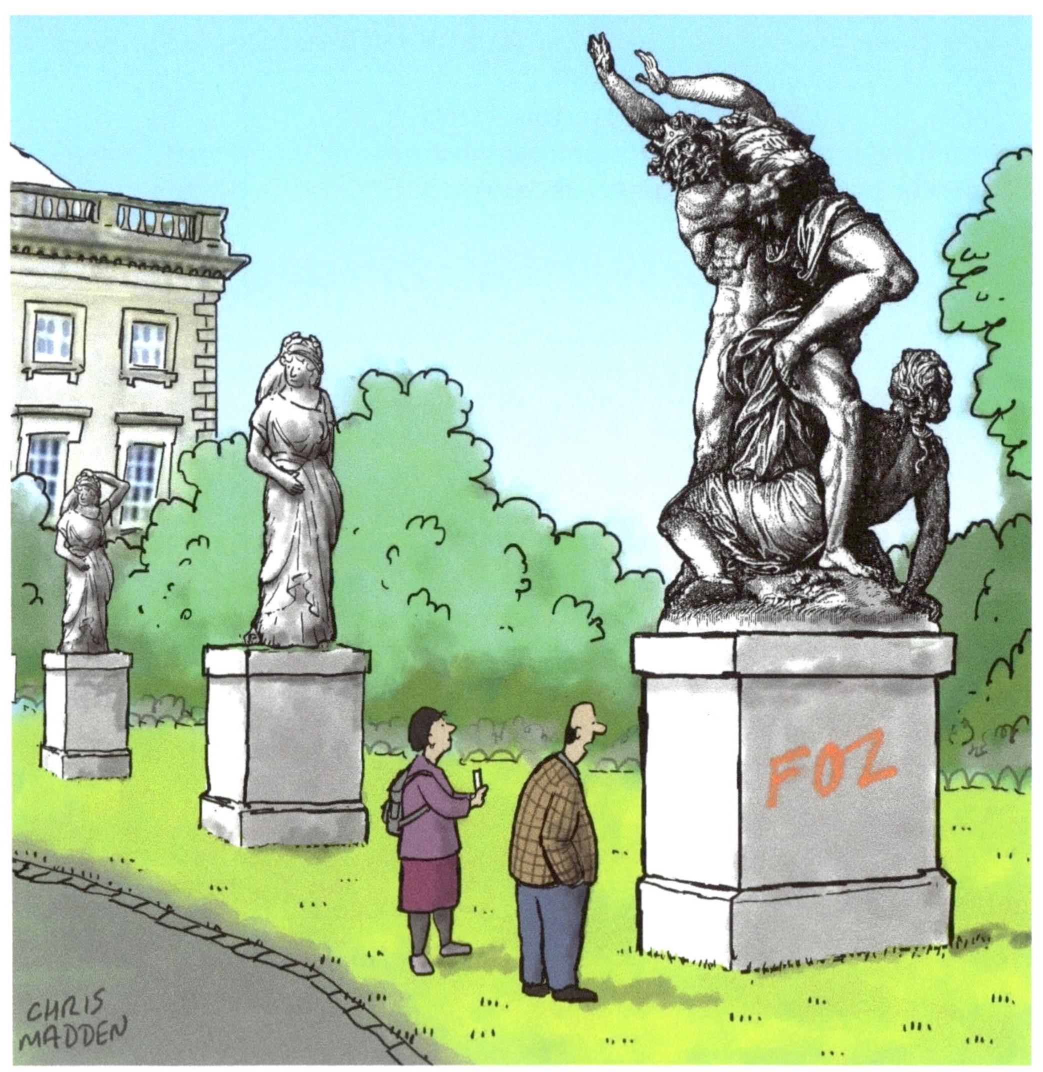

"This one's signed."

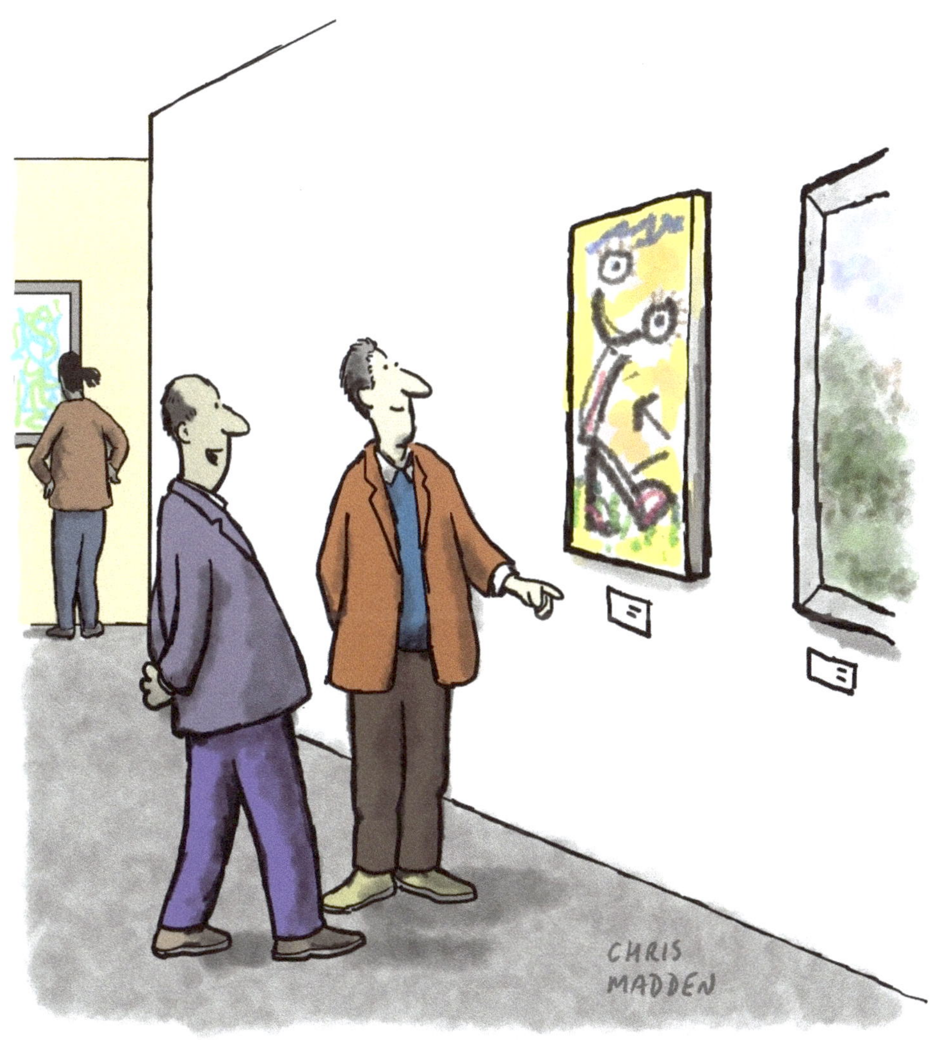

"Never mind the quality – just look at the meaning!"

"Your problem is that you're completely lacking in any form of neurosis or psychosis – you'll never make a great artist."

"How does that make you feel?"

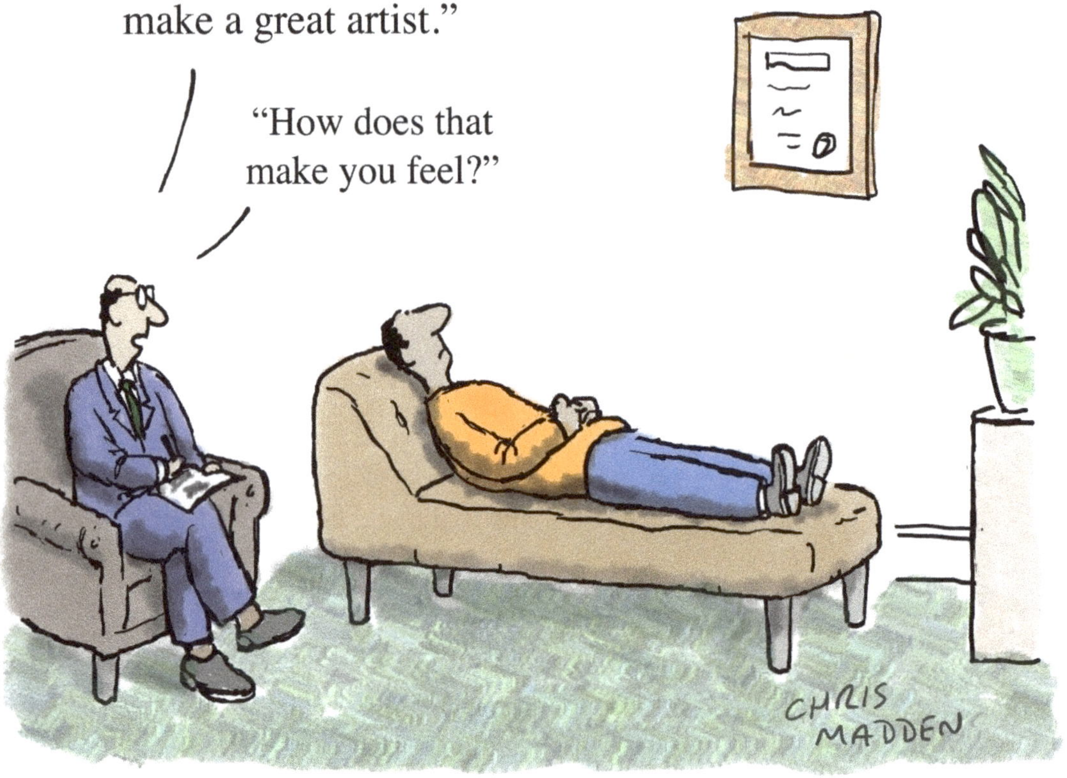

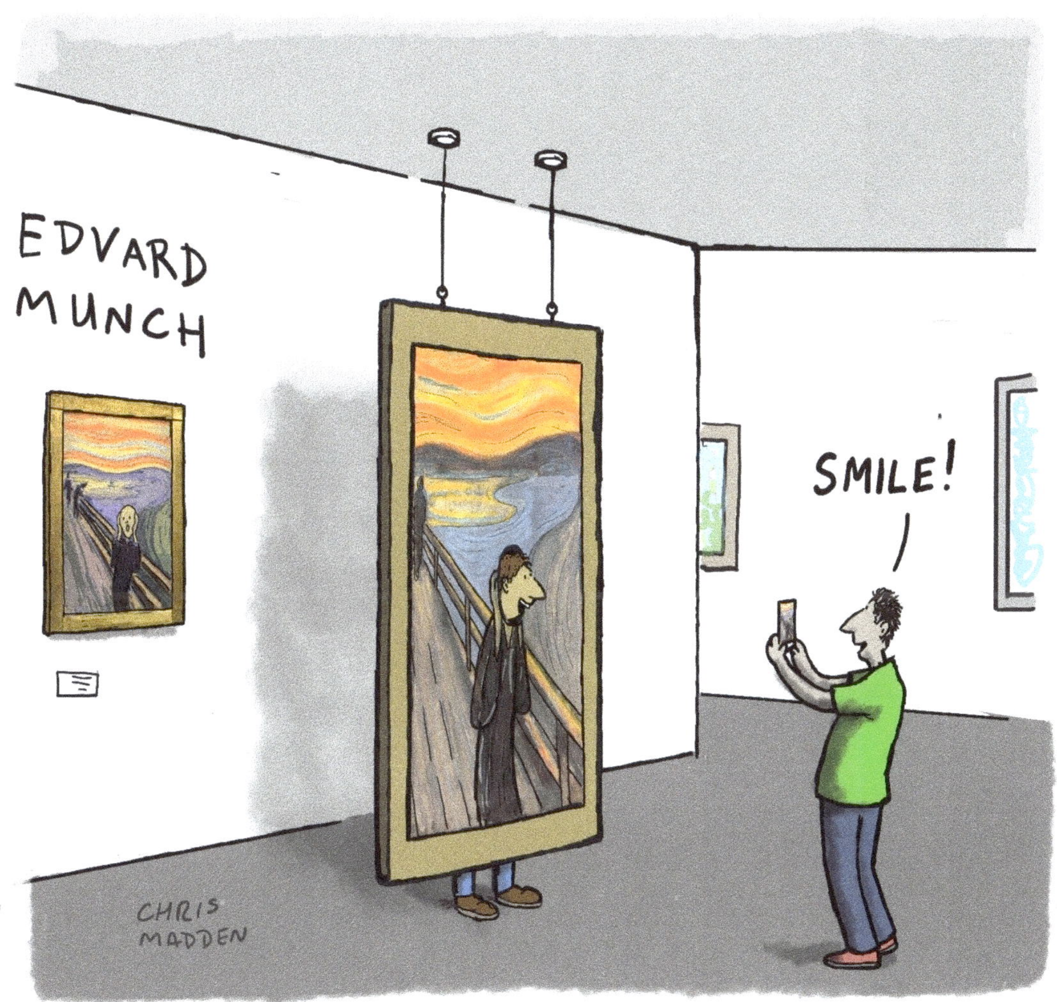
EDVARD MUNCH
SMILE!
CHRIS MADDEN

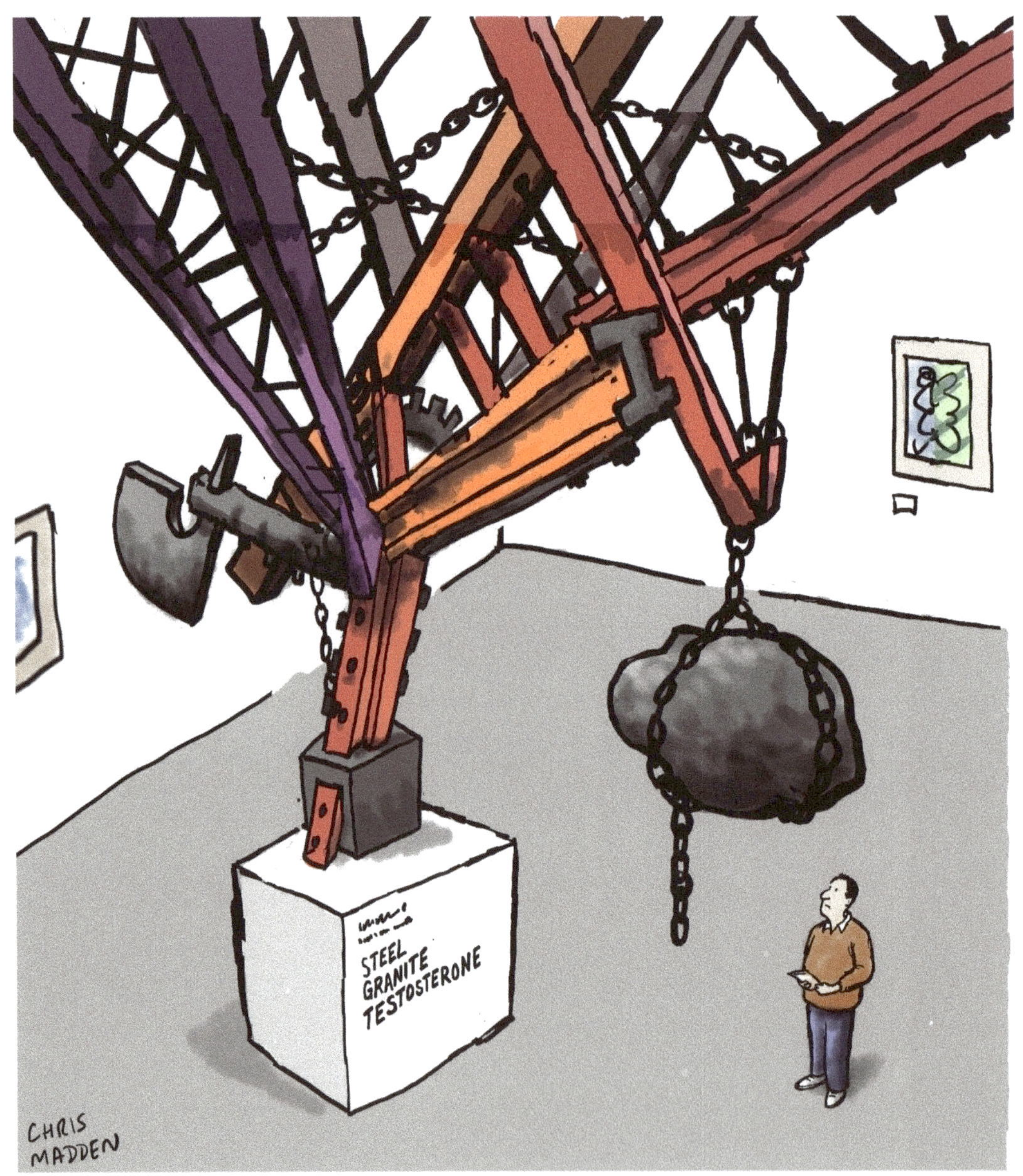
STEEL
GRANITE
TESTOSTERONE
CHRIS
MADDEN

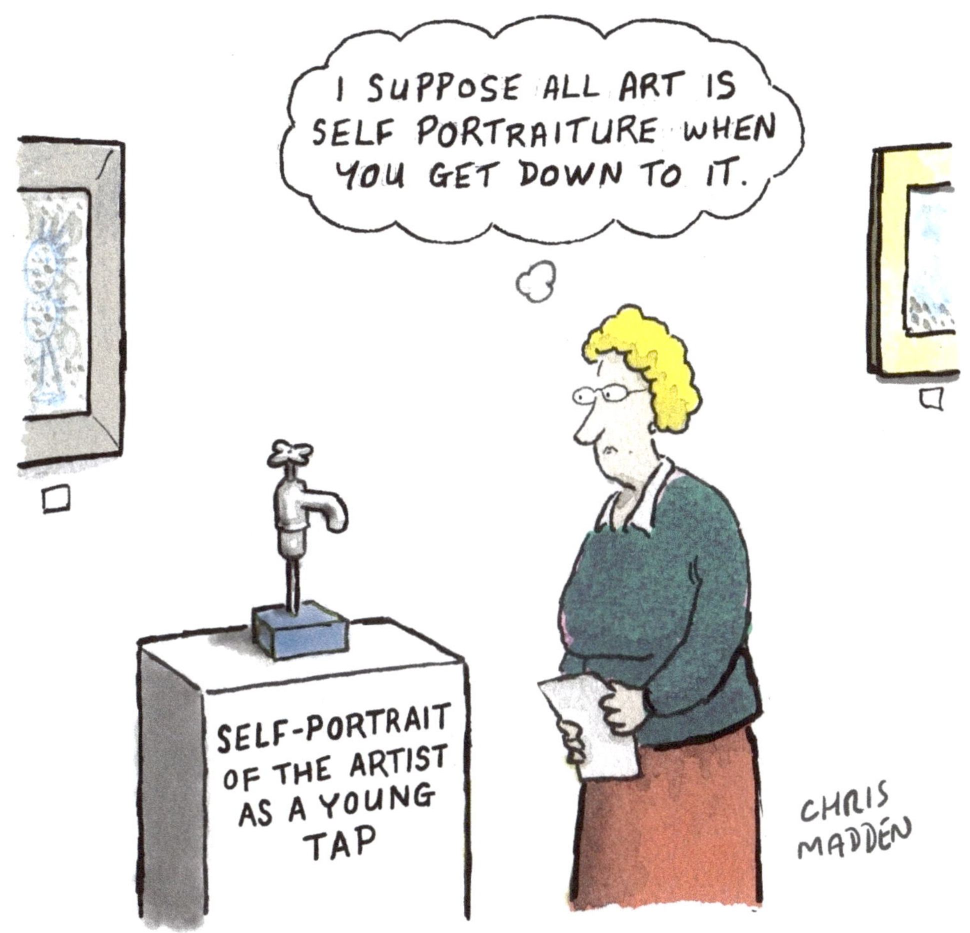
I SUPPOSE ALL ART IS SELF PORTRAITURE WHEN YOU GET DOWN TO IT.
SELF-PORTRAIT OF THE ARTIST AS A YOUNG TAP
CHRIS MADDEN

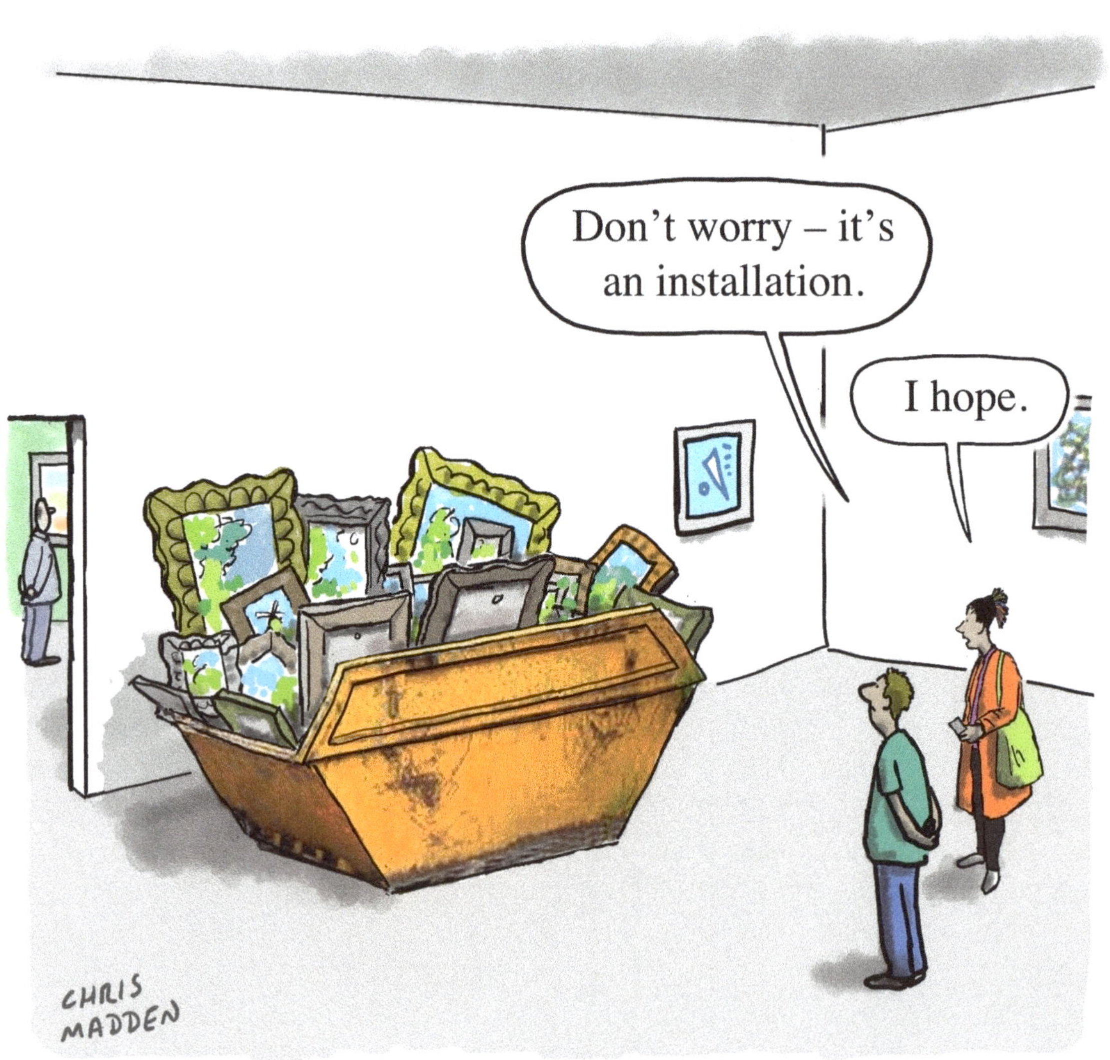
Don't worry – it's an installation.
I hope.
CHRIS MADDEN

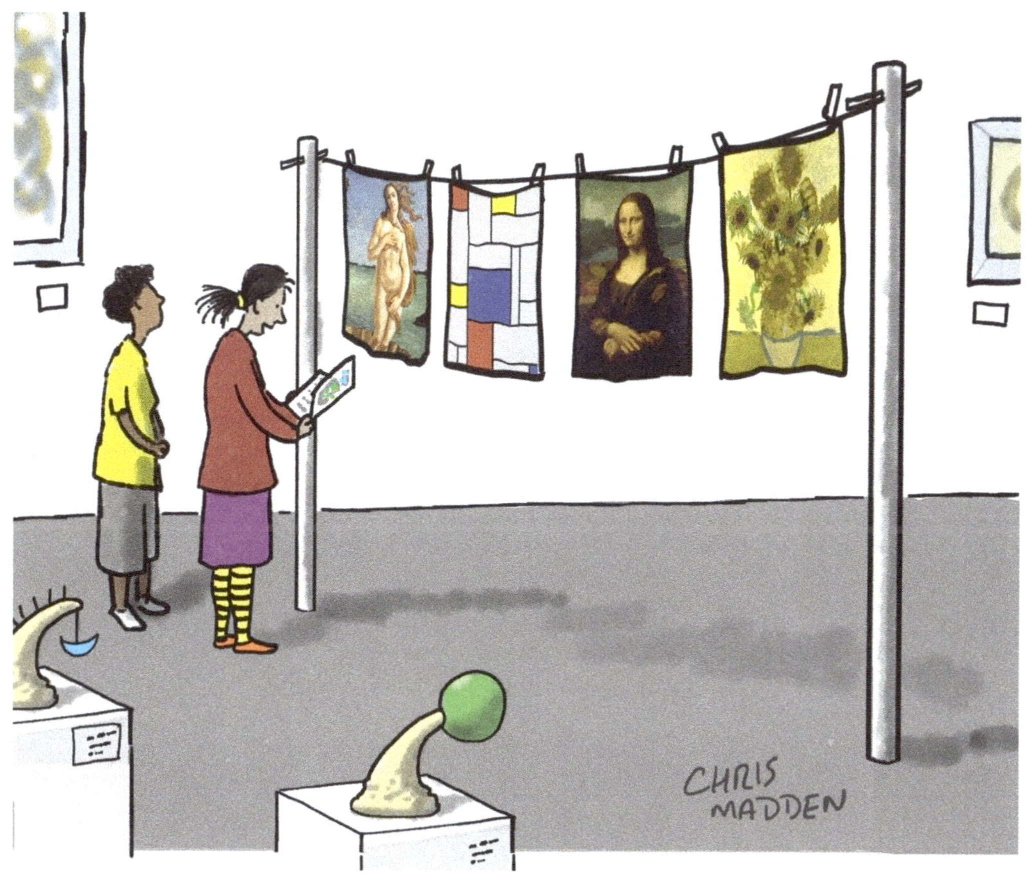

"It's called *Souvenir Tea Towels on Washing Line* and it's a comment on the way that the men get to create the memorable art while the women do the washing up."

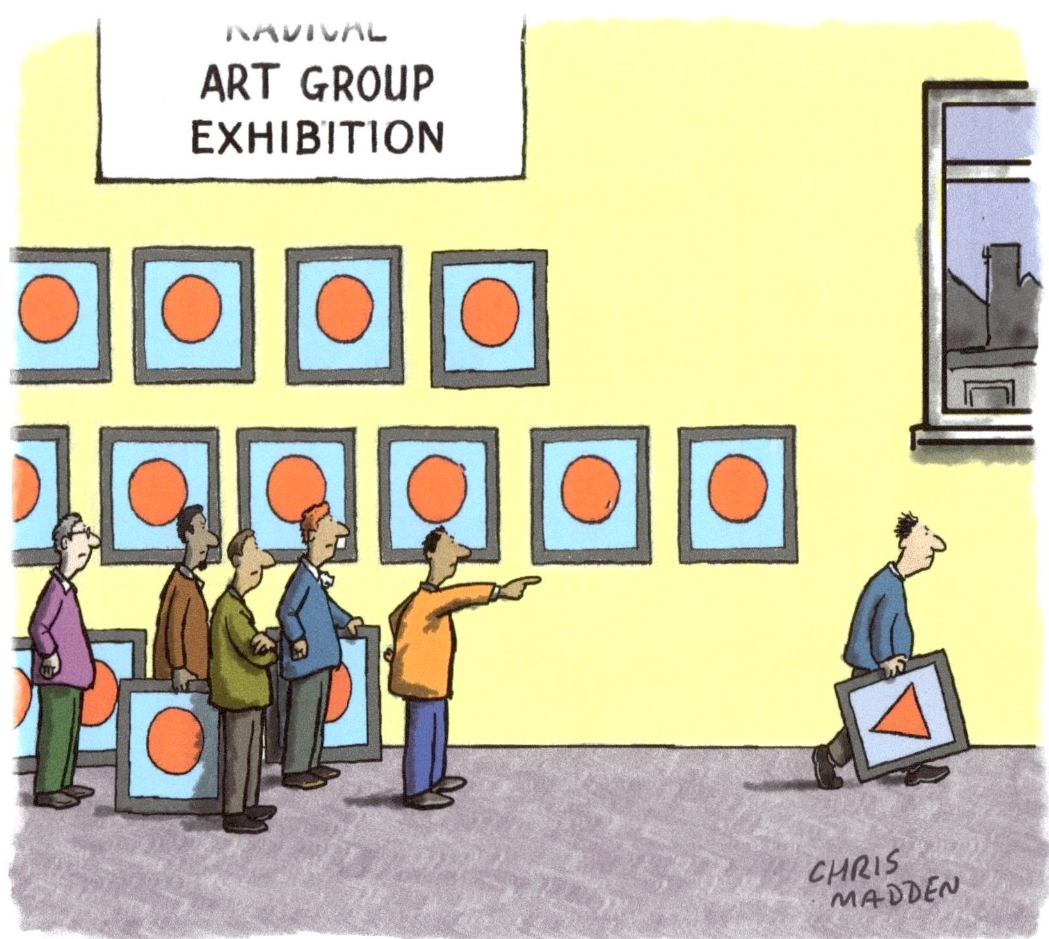
ART GROUP
EXHIBITION
CHRIS
MADDEN

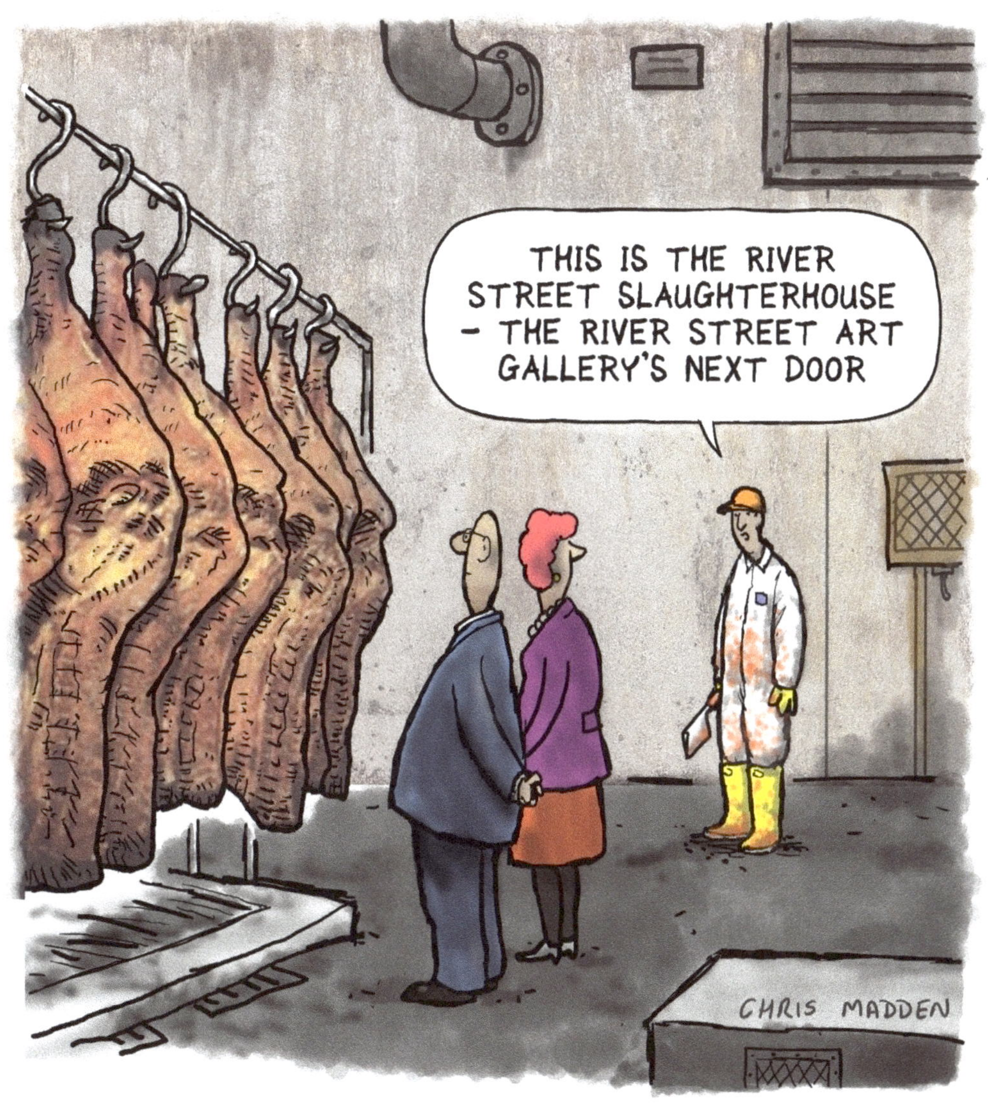
THIS IS THE RIVER STREET SLAUGHTERHOUSE - THE RIVER STREET ART GALLERY'S NEXT DOOR
CHRIS MADDEN

UNUSUAL ART TECHNIQUES

USING HAND FANS TO CREATE SMOKE SCULPTURES.

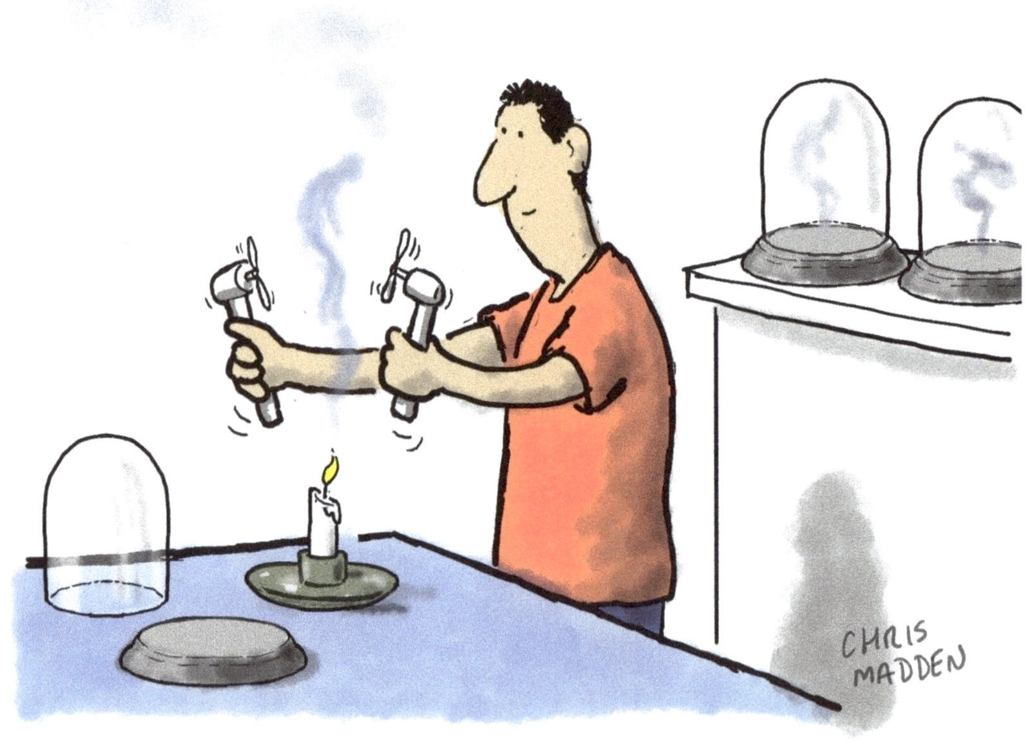

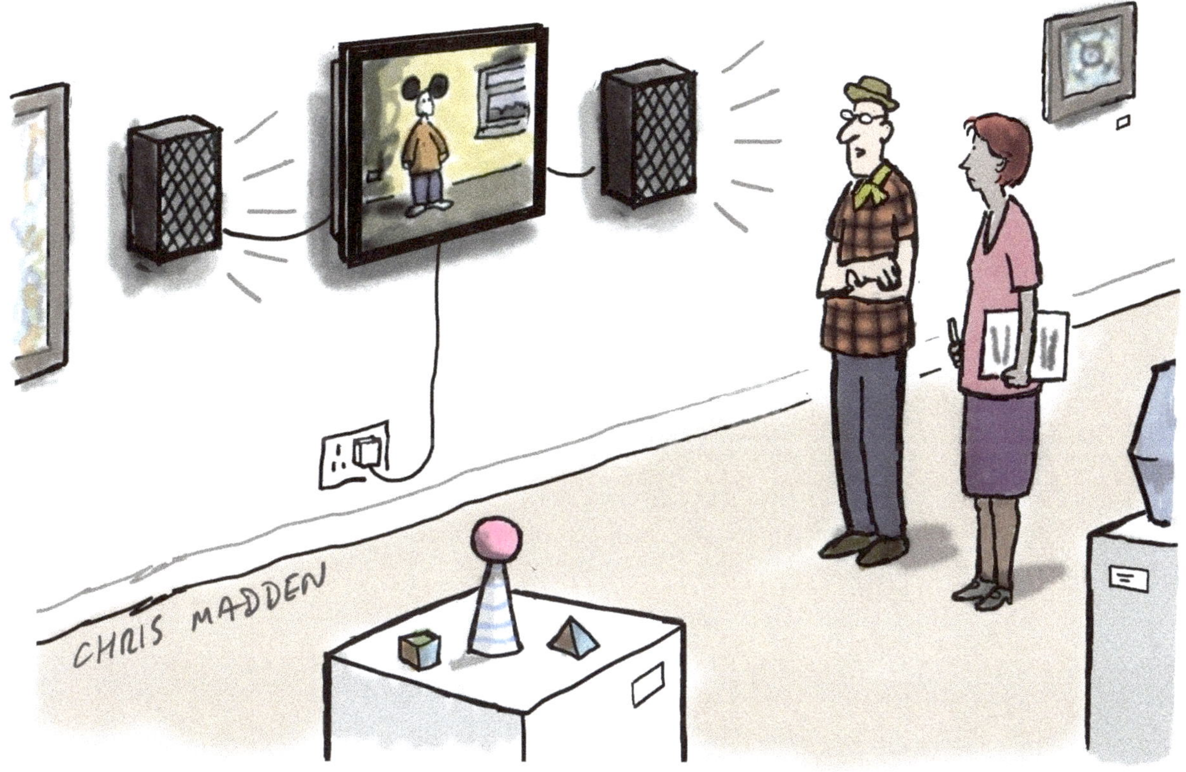

"The soundtrack to my video piece has nothing to do with the subject matter. It's there solely to annoy people when they're looking at other artists' work."

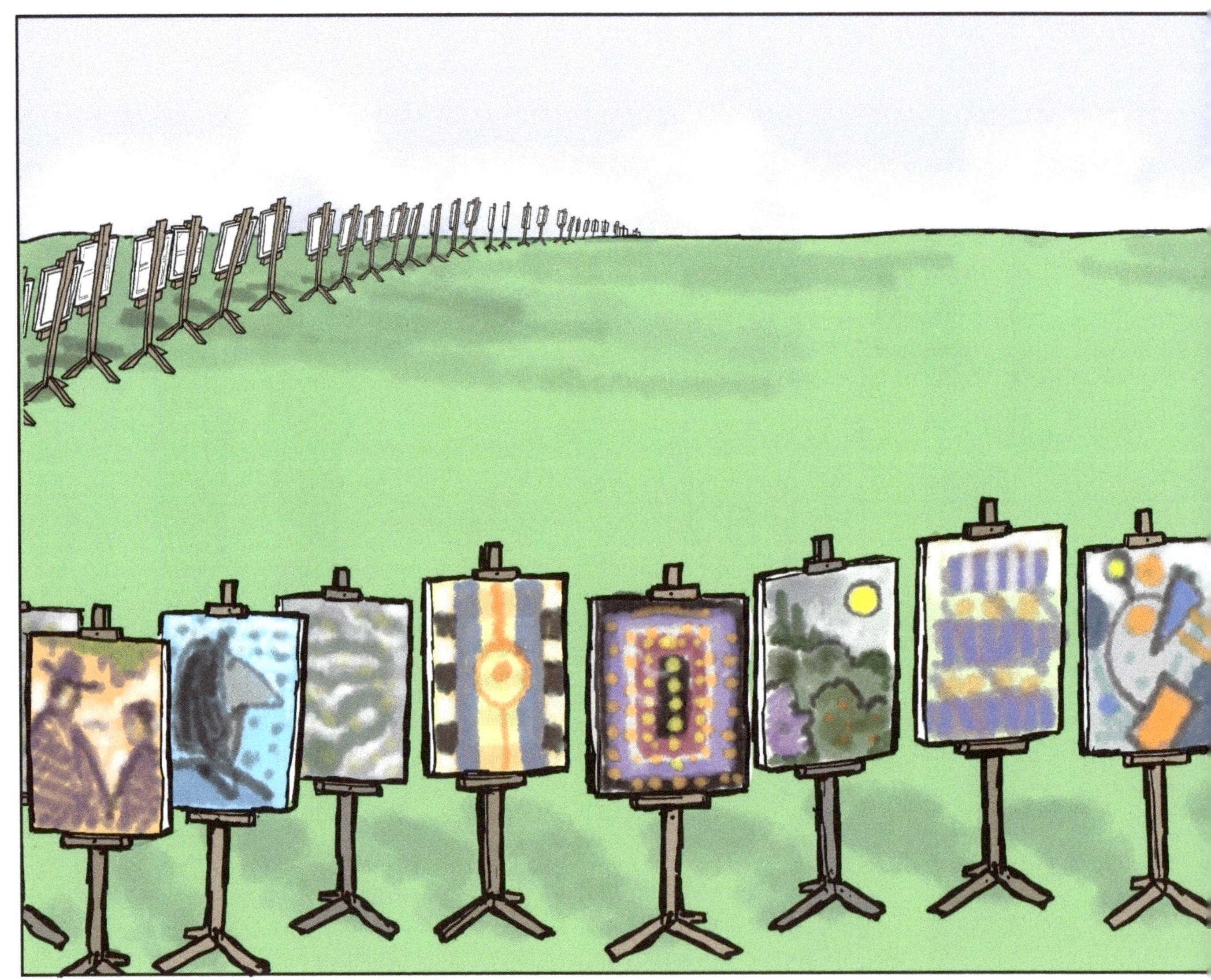

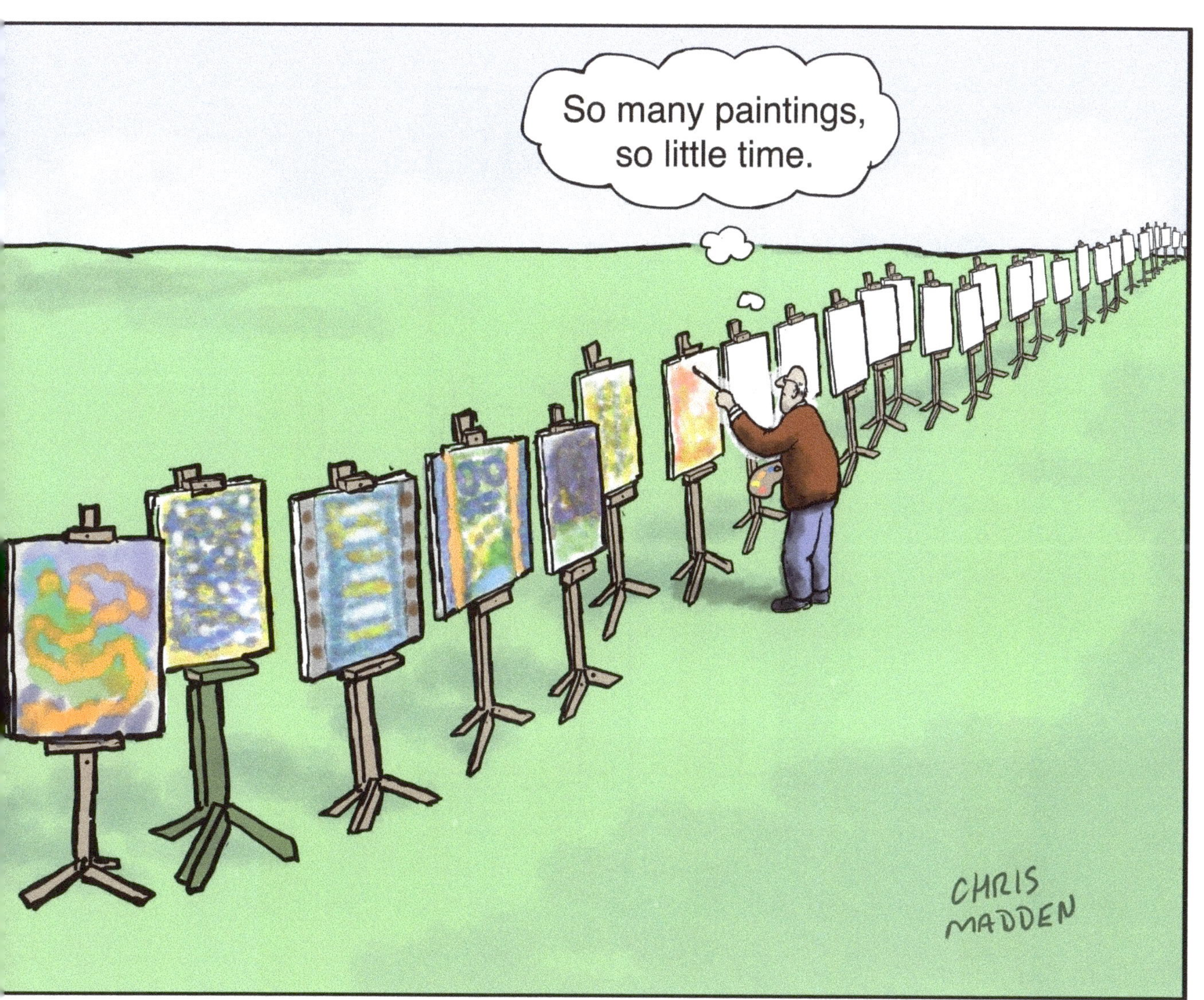
So many paintings, so little time.
CHRIS MADDEN

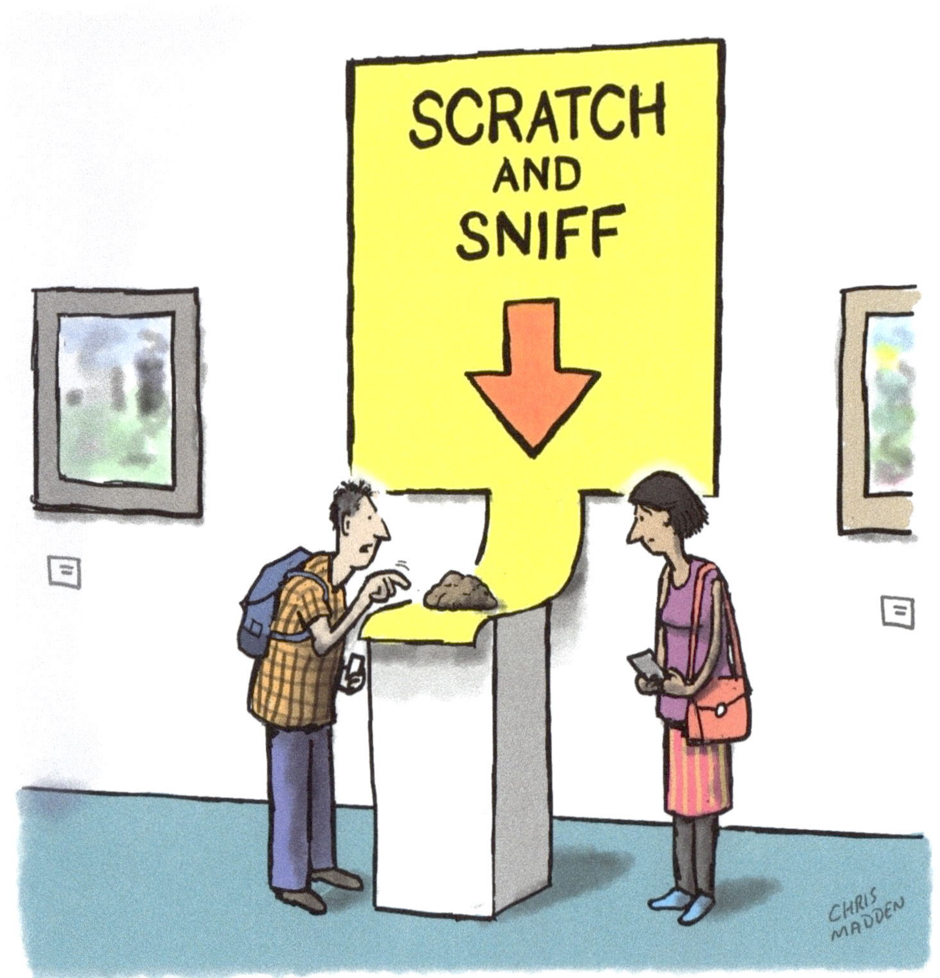

"It smells of gimmickry."

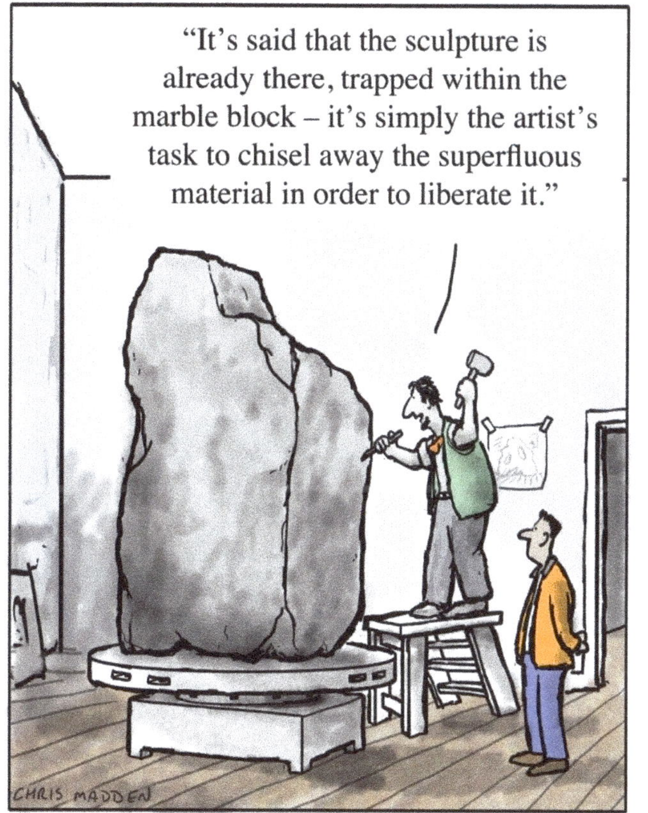
"It's said that the sculpture is already there, trapped within the marble block – it's simply the artist's task to chisel away the superfluous material in order to liberate it."
CHRIS MADDEN

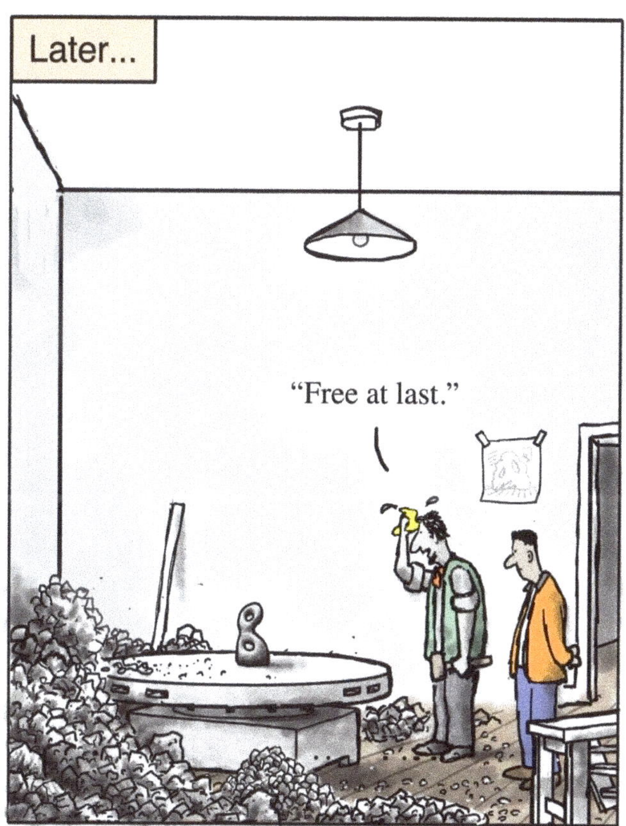
Later...
"Free at last."

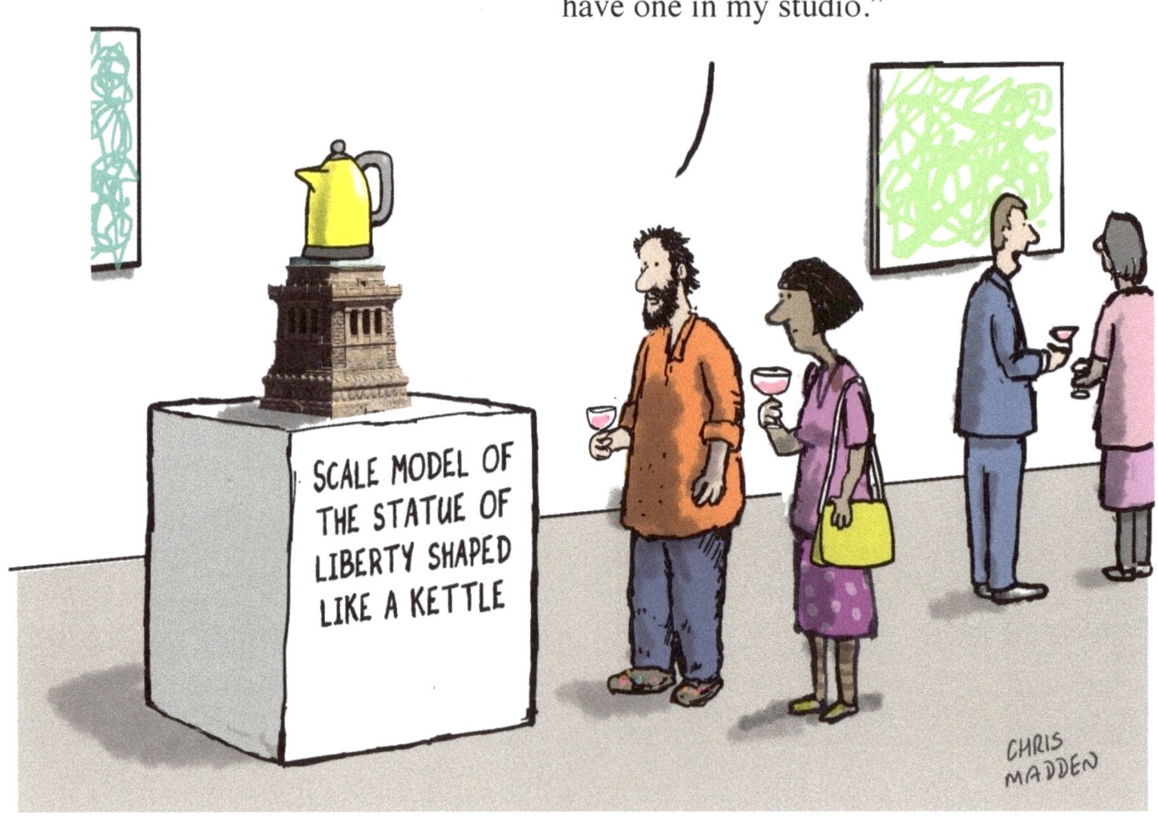

"I was going to use a frying pan but I didn't have one in my studio."

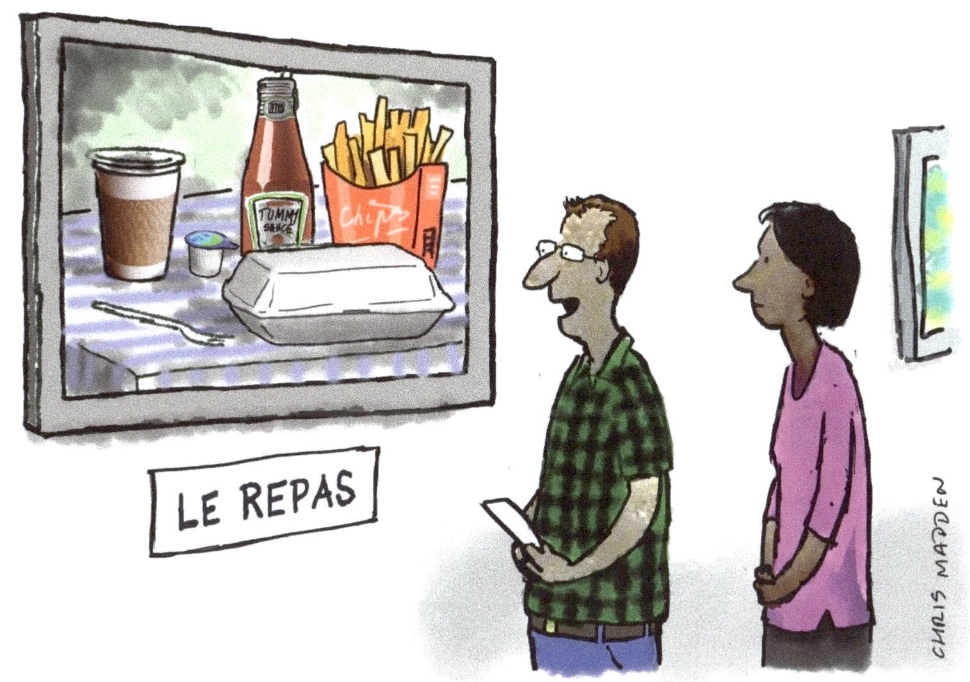

"Incredible brushwork – just look how exquisitely she's captured the light on the polystyrene!"

DO NOT CROSS LINE

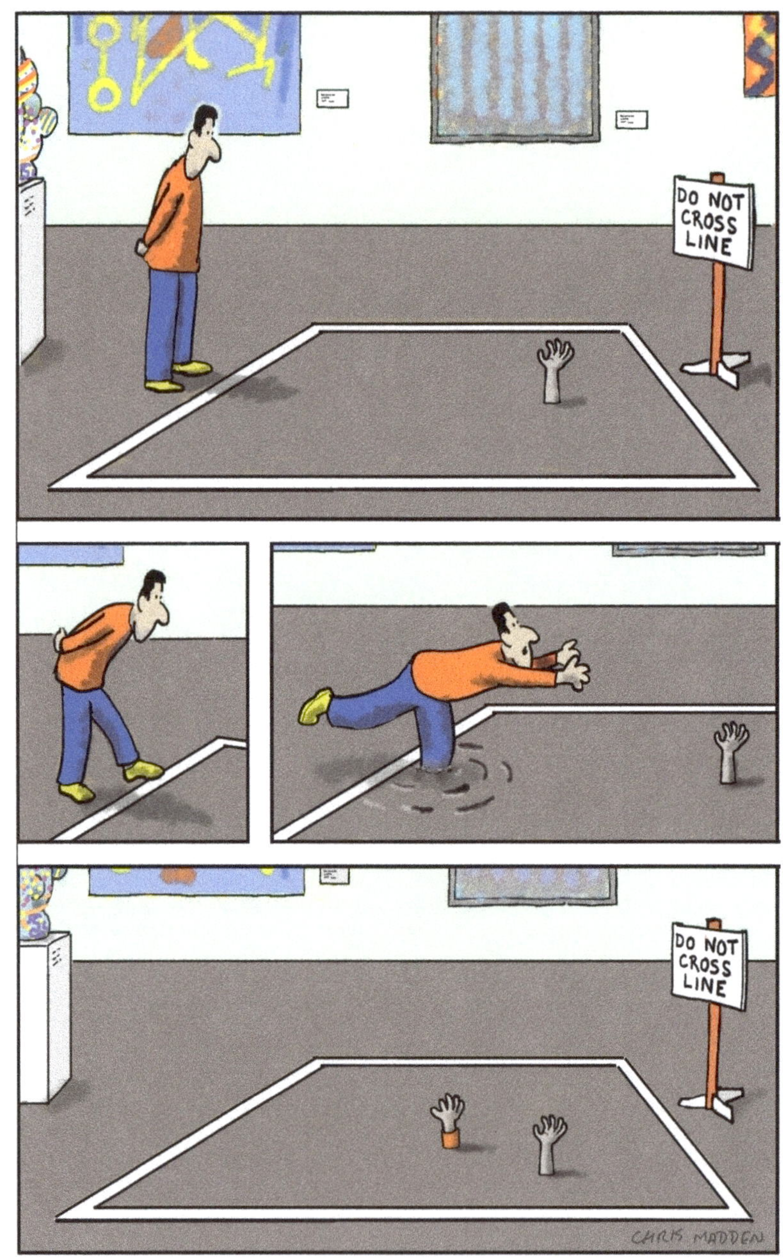

Later...

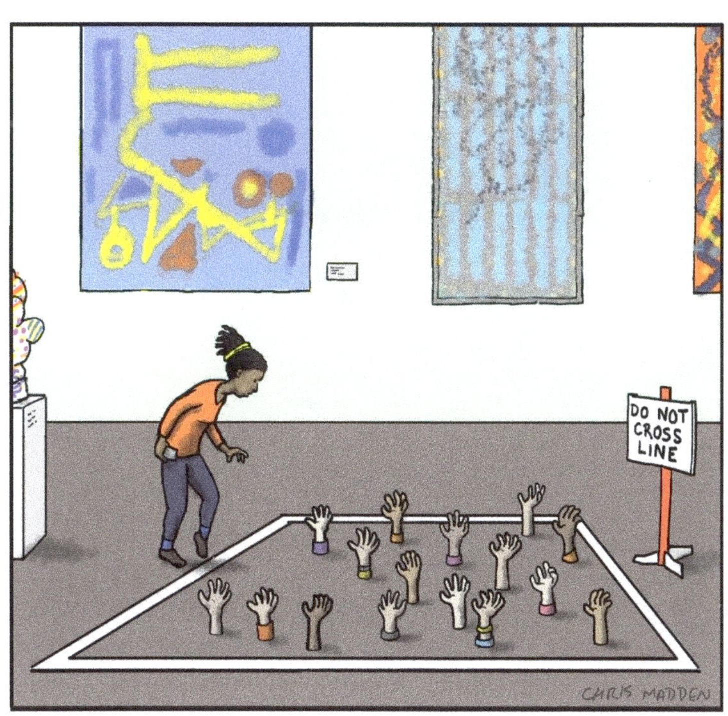

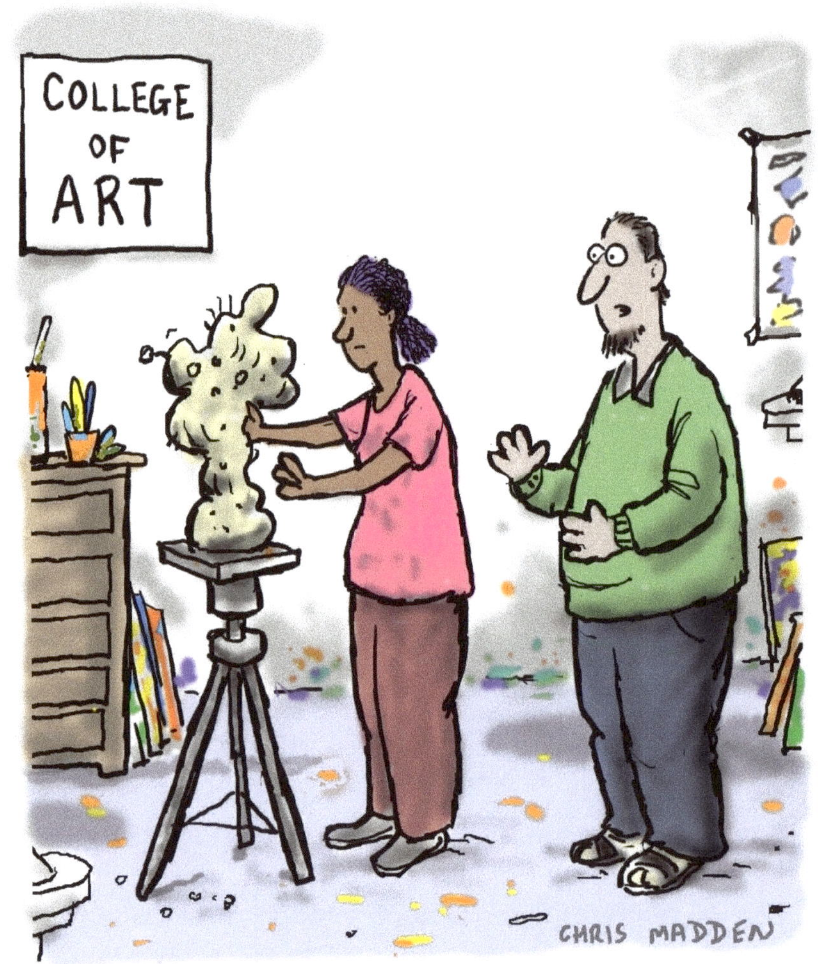

"No, no, no, Kimberley! To be artistically valid you must work from a position of deep understanding of art's role in questioning the aesthetic and intellectual norms of the prevailing cultural zeitgeist – you can't just go off with some crazy idea of your own!"

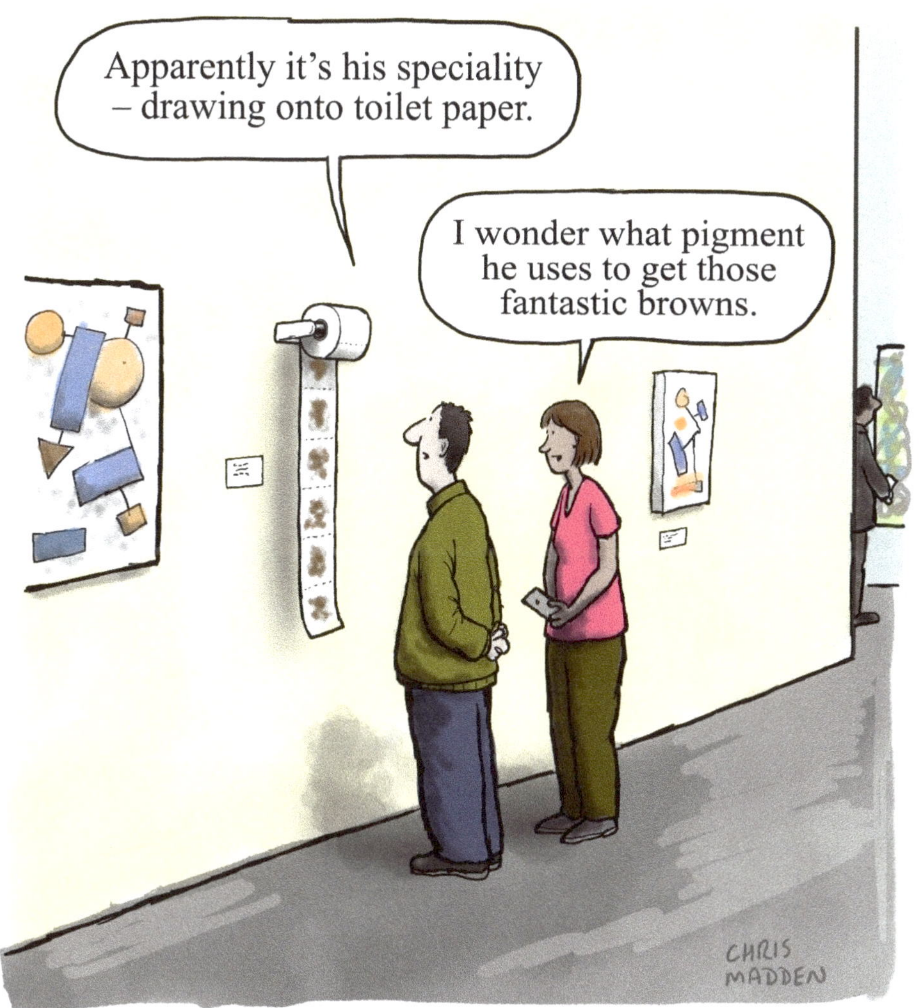
Apparently it's his speciality – drawing onto toilet paper.
I wonder what pigment he uses to get those fantastic browns.
CHRIS MADDEN

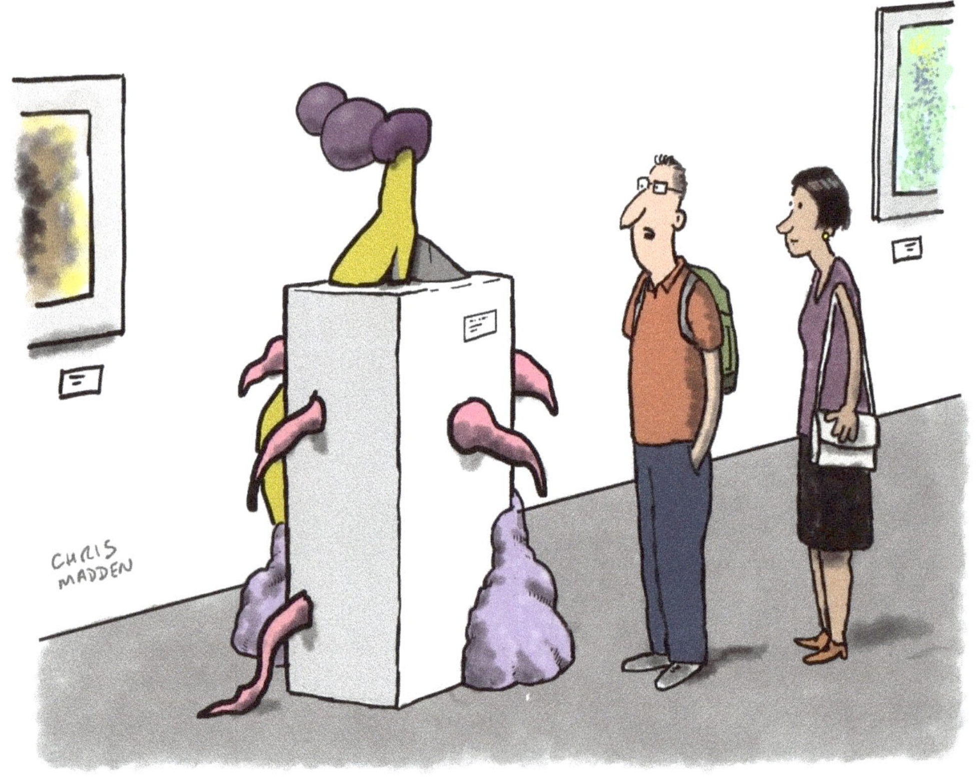

"Fantastic – that's such an eloquent critique of contemporary post-colonial neo-liberal society!"

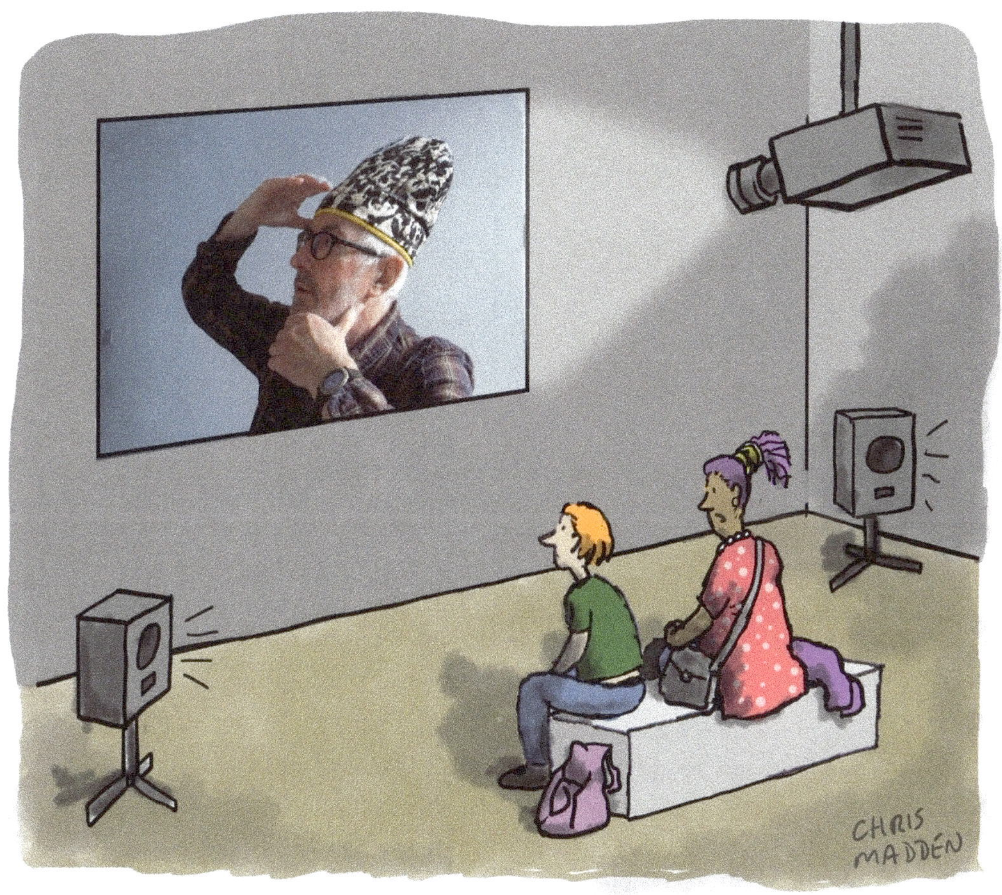

“You’re new to video art, aren’t you? Well, think of it as an initiation rite into contemporary art through ‘ordeal by boredom’.”

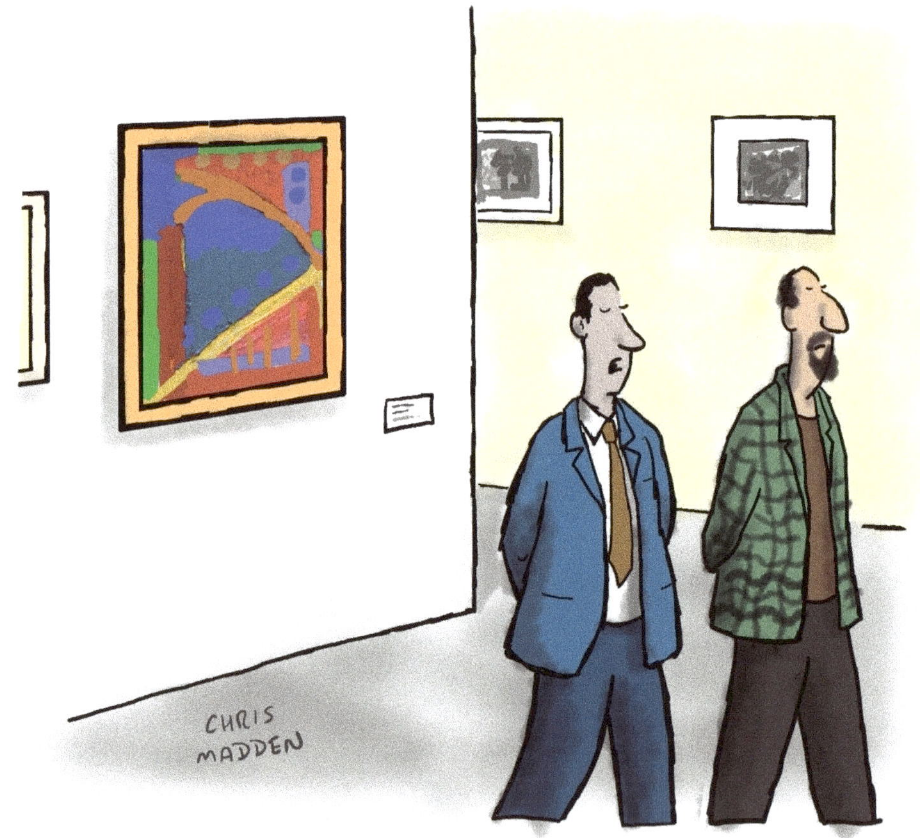

"His work is much too pleasant to be taken seriously."

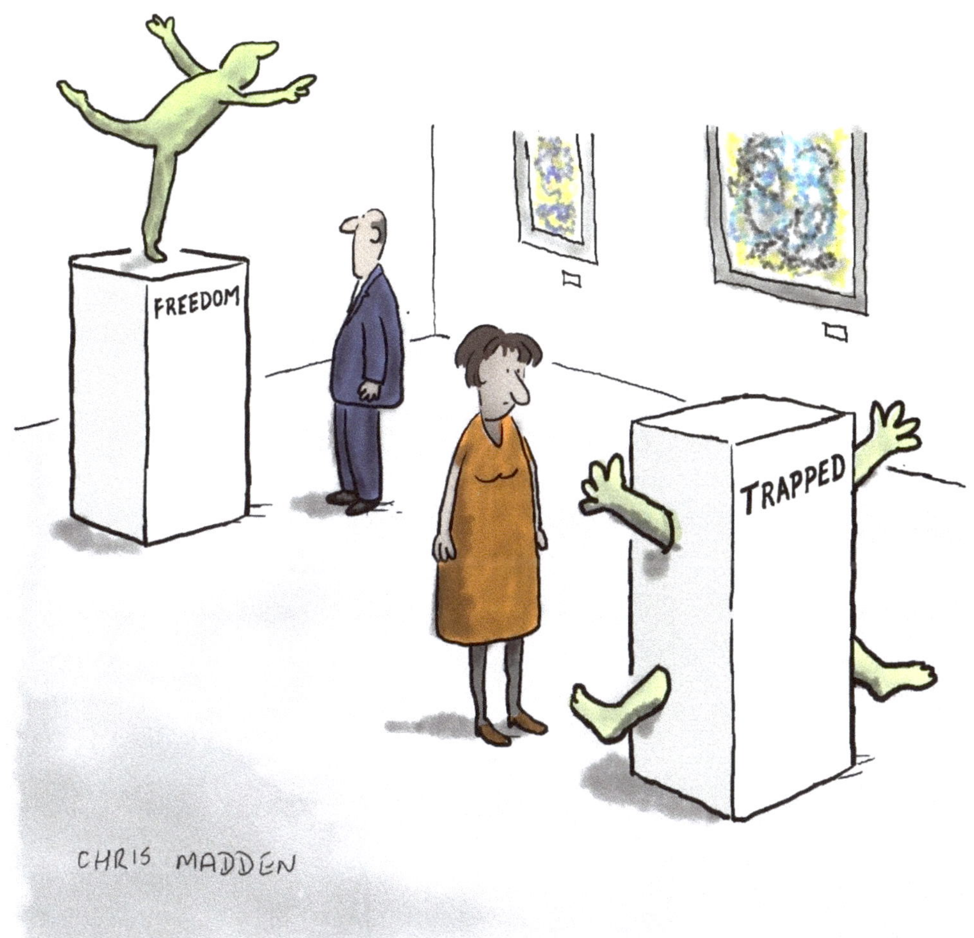
FREEDOM
TRAPPED
CHRIS MADDEN

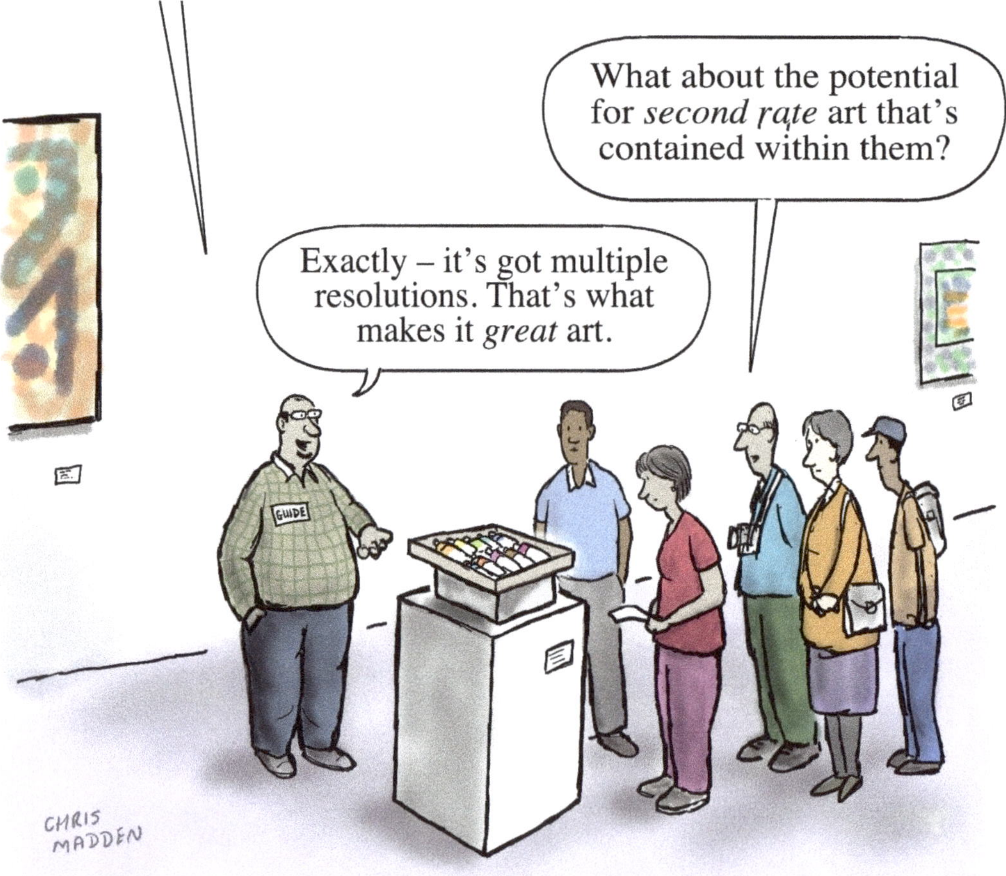
Here the artist is exhibiting a set of unopened tubes of paint. They signify the *potential* for great art that is contained within them.
Exactly – it's got multiple resolutions. That's what makes it *great* art.
What about the potential for *second rate* art that's contained within them?
GUIDE
CHRIS MADDEN

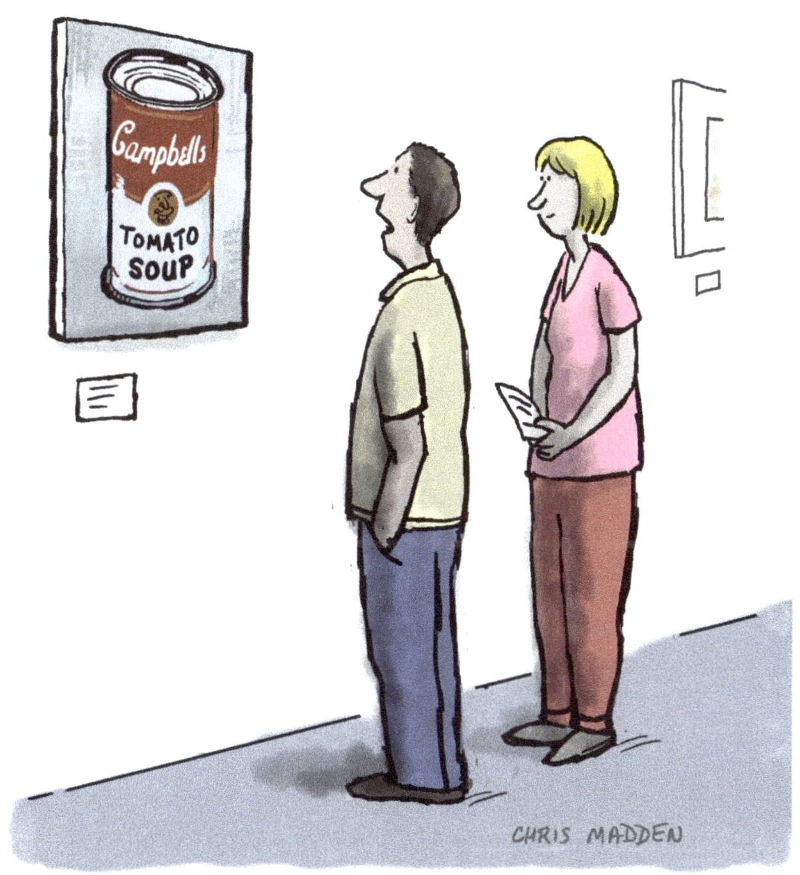

"It's rumoured that he did a series of Heinz soup tins too, but the whole lot were bought by Campbells and were never seen again."

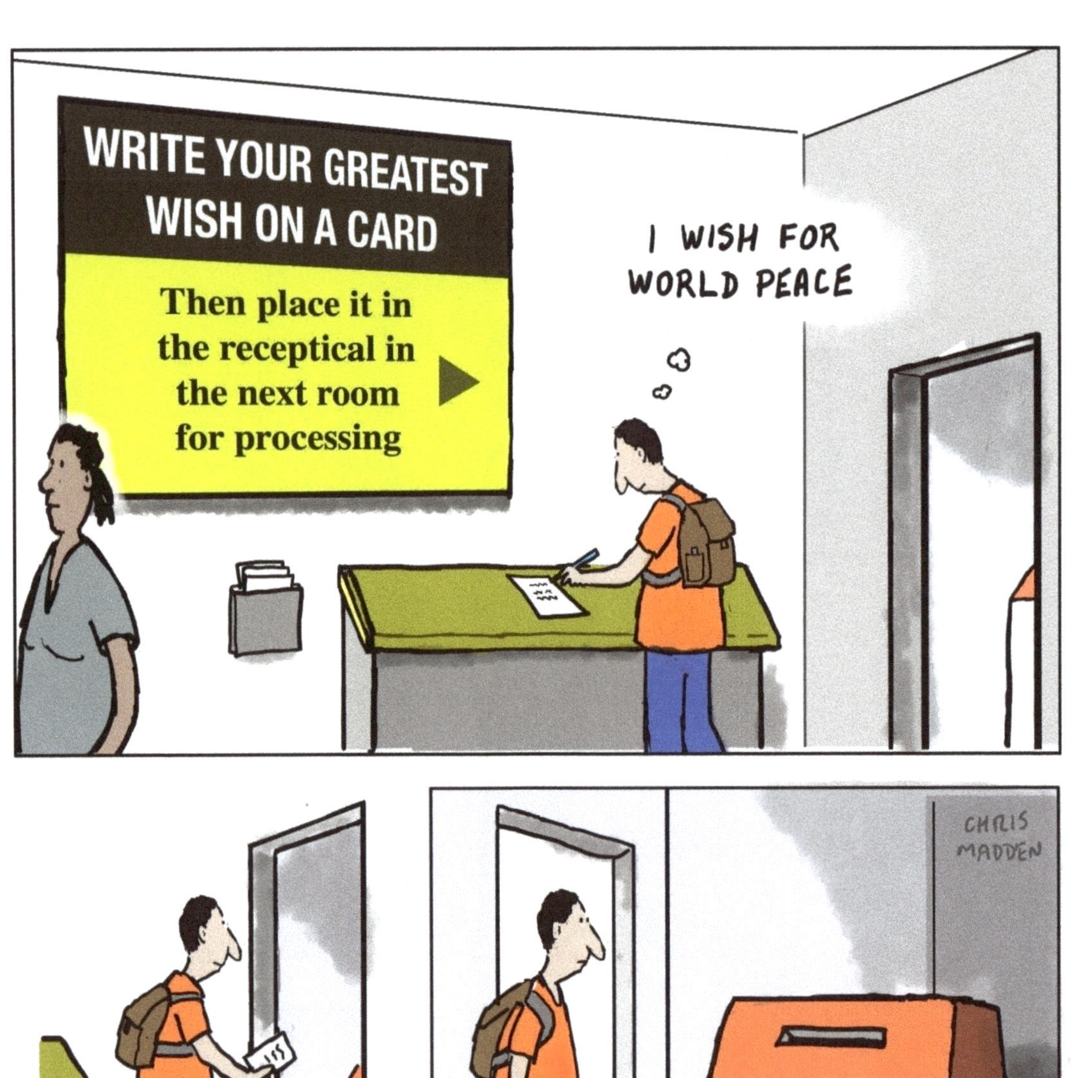
WRITE YOUR GREATEST WISH ON A CARD
Then place it in the receptical in the next room for processing
I WISH FOR WORLD PEACE
CHRIS MADDEN
SHREDDER

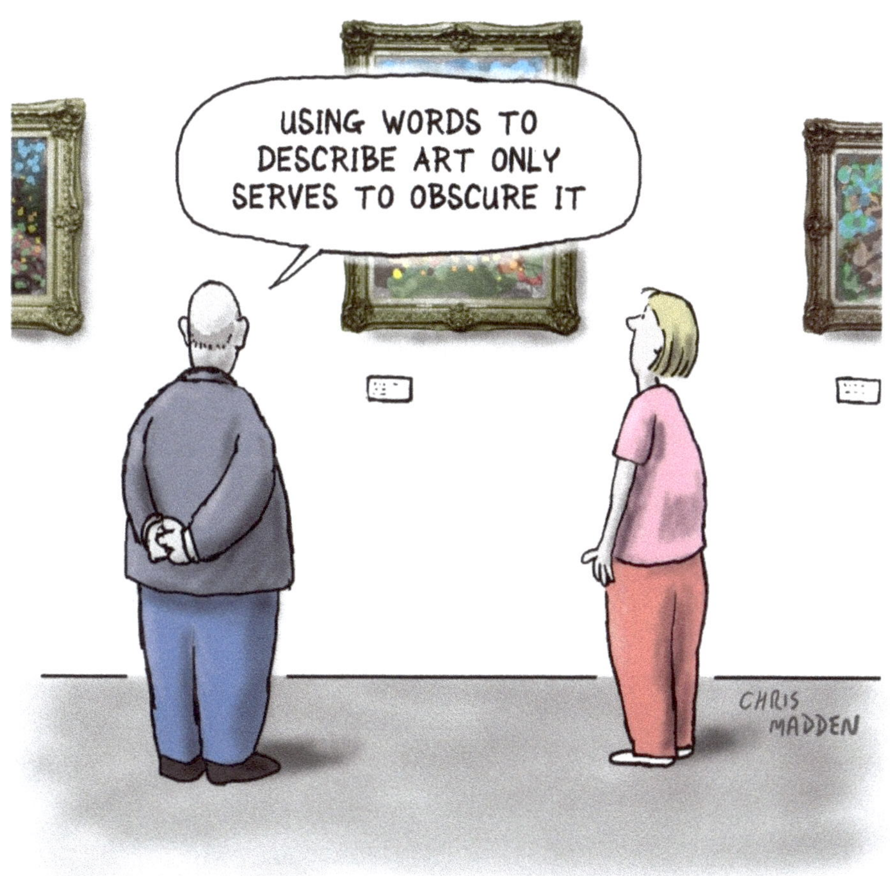
USING WORDS TO DESCRIBE ART ONLY SERVES TO OBSCURE IT
CHRIS MADDEN

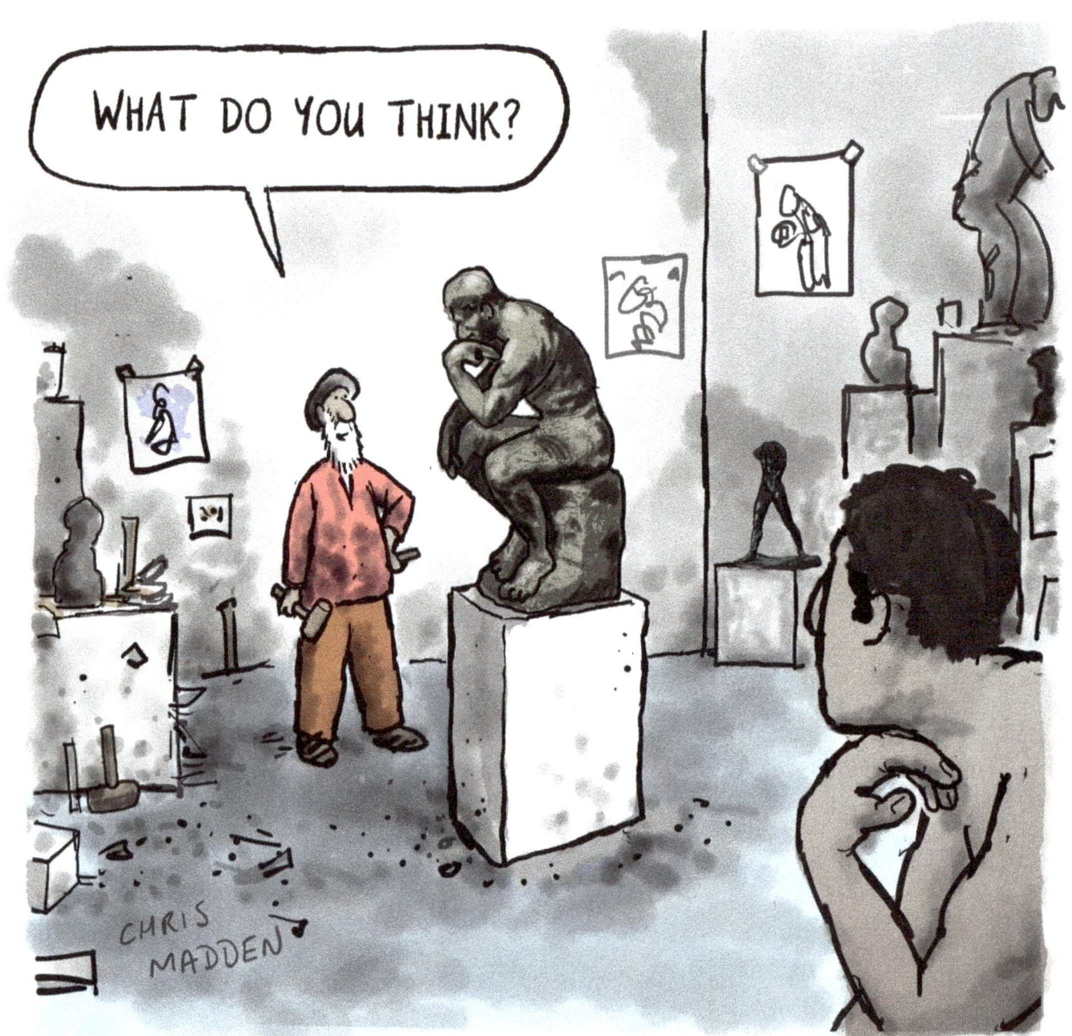
WHAT DO YOU THINK?
CHRIS MADDEN

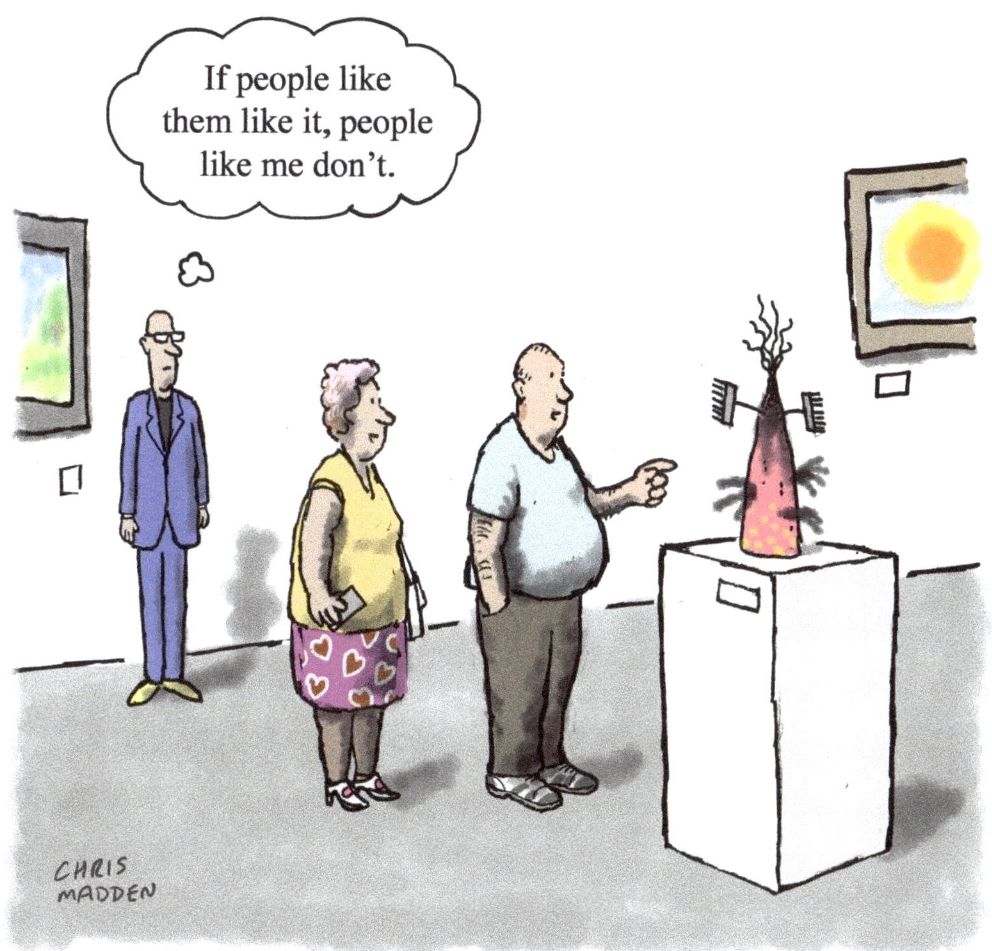
If people like
them like it, people
like me don't.
CHRIS
MADDEN

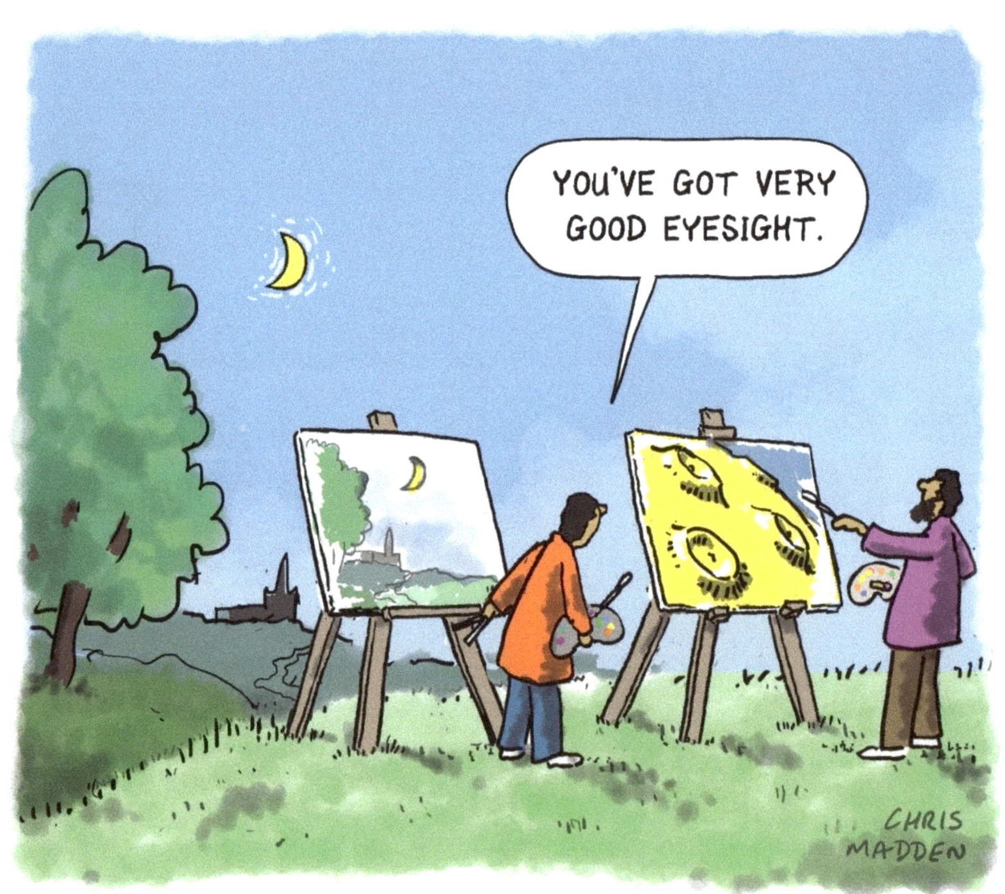
YOU'VE GOT VERY GOOD EYESIGHT.
CHRIS MADDEN

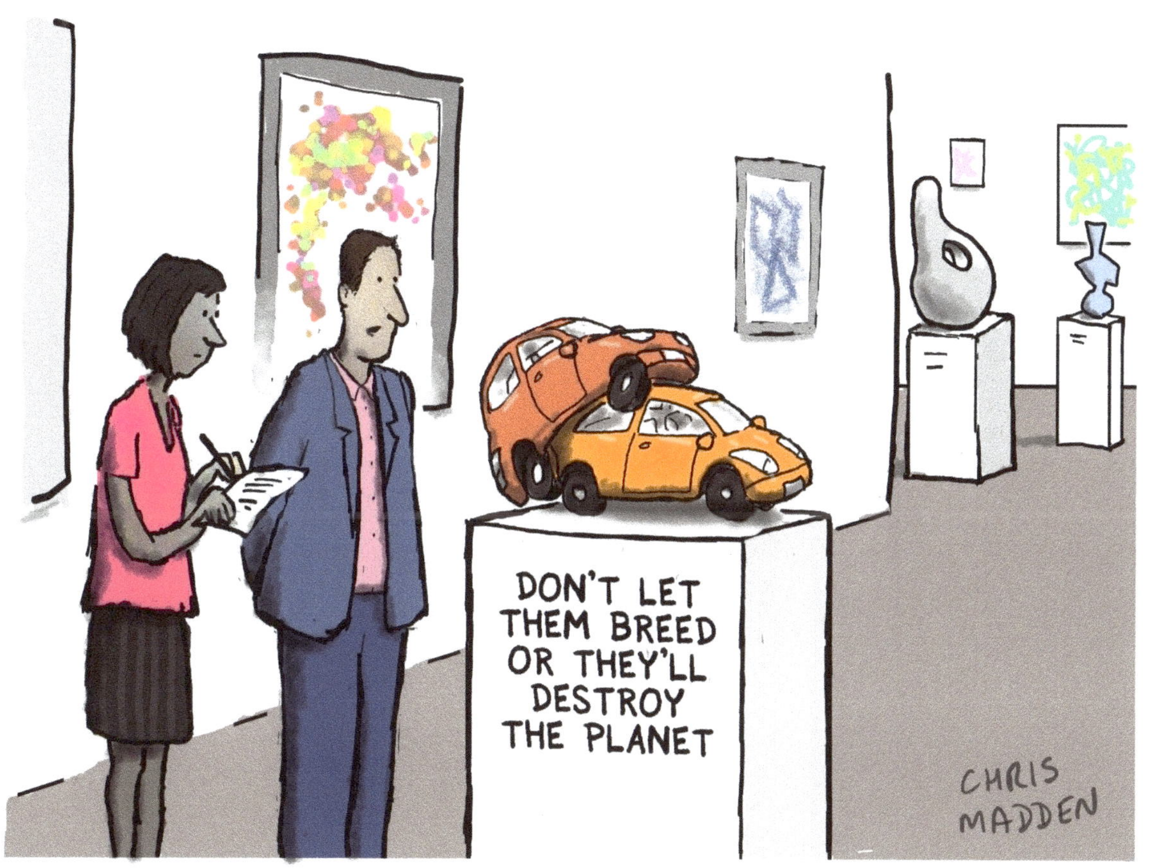

"The gallery's new sponsor is a car manufacturer, so this piece had better go into storage."

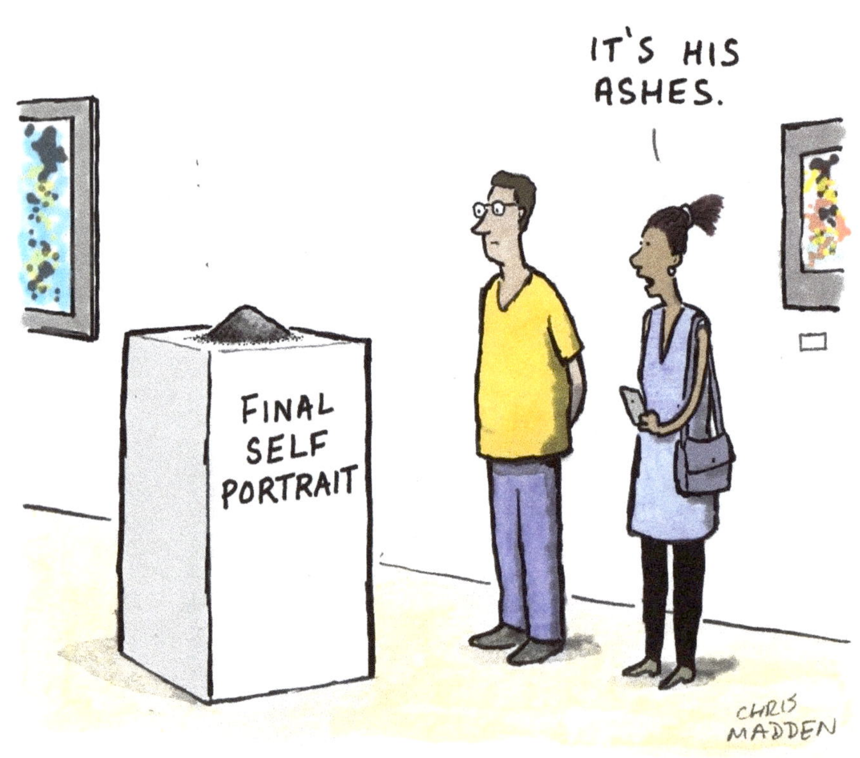
IT'S HIS ASHES.
FINAL SELF PORTRAIT
CHRIS MADDEN

www.ingramcontent.com/pod-product-compliance
Lightning Source LLC
LaVergne TN
LVHW060640110826
845147LV00018B/1016

* 9 7 8 0 9 5 4 8 5 5 1 7 8 *